GOING BACK
TO WORK

WORK
W O R K
OF

Washing Time
Booker T Jones
Duke Ellington
Blues For New Orleans
BFNO

Made Me Get Rid Of Records

Free Space

Reached out to people

Doing Art CD's Secary

If you want to know how...

**Essential Computing Skills for Working Women or
Returners**
*Everything you need to know to use computers
in the workplace*

Can be used before making a job application and later at
your desk; to prepare, give confidence and keep up-to-date.

The Job Application Handbook
*Proven strategies and effective techniques for selling
yourself to an employer*

'A great buy. It reiterates points which need to be repeated
and gives practical advice on job finding.'
– *Office Secretary Magazine*

Write a Winning CV
*Essential CV writing skills that will get you the job
you want*

'If you are in the market for advice, *Write a Winning CV* is a
great starting point.' – The *Guardian*

howtobooks

Send for a free copy of the latest catalogue to:

How To Books
Spring Hill House,
Spring Hill Road, Begbroke,
Oxford OX5 1RX, United Kingdom
email: info@howtobooks.co.uk
http://www.howtobooks.co.uk

GOING BACK TO WORK

A practical guide to re-entering the job market

"An absolute must for anyone who is beginning this new phase of life."
INSTITUTE OF MANAGEMENT

SALLY LONGSON

howtobooks

Published by How To Books Ltd,
Spring Hill House, Spring Hill Road,
Begbroke, Oxford OX5 1RX. United Kingdom.
Tel: (01865) 375794. Fax: (01865) 379162.
email: info@howtobooks.co.uk
http://www.howtobooks.co.uk

British Library Cataloguing in Publication Data
A catalogue record for this book is available from the British Library

ISBN 10: 1 84528 075 X
ISBN 13: 978 1 84528 075 8

Produced for How To Books by Deer Park Productions, Tavistock
Typeset by PDQ Typesetting, Newcastle-under-Lyme, Staffs.
Cover design by Baseline Arts Ltd, Oxford
Printed and bound in Great Britain by Bell & Bain Ltd, Glasgow

NOTE: The material contained in this book is set out in good faith for
general guidance and no liability can be accepted for loss or expense
incurred as a result of relying in particular circumstances on
statements made in the book. The laws and regulations are complex
and liable to change, and readers should check the current position
with the relevant authorities before making personal arrangements.

Contents

Illustrations

Preface

If you've picked up this book, it's a sure sign that a change is on the horizon for you. You're about to return to work.

You're not alone. Every year, thousands of people go back to work after a break. A return can enable you to earn a living, to boost your finances, to meet the challenge, to make a difference, to enhance your own confidence, development and self-esteem; to be seen as an individual in your own right, rather than somebody's partner, carer or parent; to learn new skills and meet new people – and to have fun.

For many, the main blocks will be their confidence levels: *'Who'd want me?'* or *'Go back to work? I wouldn't know where to start!'* But there are more opportunities now than ever before to return to work and retrain, whether you want to set up on your own or work for someone else.

Like anything in life, you get out of this book what you put into it, so make the most of the assessment exercises, designed to help you work out what you want from work. This book focuses on *you* and what you want. It does not cover care for dependants in any detail, although it will point you in the direction of help and support. You have a right to a fulfilling life, and to work you love and believe in and while Chapters 1 to 8 will help you assess what you want to do, Chapters 9 to 18 will help you go out there and make it happen.

Look on your return to work as a challenge to rise to and an adventure to enjoy. And be inspired by Tennyson:

> Come, my friends.
> 'Tis never too late to seek a newer world.

Sally Longson

1

What's Your Motive?

⟨It's time to think about yourself and what you want in life.⟩

Life is like a book, containing a series of chapters which all link together and create their own life story. Some chapters are straightforward, while others – especially those involving careers, relationships and parenthood – offer more of a challenge. Inevitably, each chapter of your life draws to a conclusion and a new one dawns.

Case study: Jane, a mother of three

'It's a funny thing, raising children. You bring them up, wanting them to be independent, able to stand on their own two feet. But when they finally leave, it's so *hard*. You just have to smile, wave them off and keep the tears to yourself for later. You know that you're moving on to another phase of your own life and that's it's time to do something about it.'

Joining the club

People take time out from work every year for many reasons, such as:

- To raise children.
- To look after dependants such as elderly relatives, or a partner.
- To travel.
- To do some voluntary work.
- To follow an interest or hobby.
- To study, either for a qualification or for the fun of it.
- Simply to take time out.
- To enjoy a lottery win or inheritance.
- They were made redundant.
- To be detained at Her Majesty's pleasure.
- They were fired.
- To try something new.
- To recover from a personal situation such as illness.
- Their company folded.
- To retire.
- To relocate with their partner.

The fact that so many people take time out and then return to work means you're not alone in this journey. It also means that employers are increasingly used to seeing breaks from employment in CVs. They will want to know how you filled your time and may ask what is motivating you to return to work and why you're doing it now. But most understand that people need and/or want to break away from the workplace to cater for family or to have time out etc. It's up to you to show them how the skills that you've acquired in that time will benefit them.

 **Making choices**

As you contemplate your return to work, you've got many choices before you, and this book will raise your awareness of some of those. For example, do you *want* to go back, or do you think you have no choice?

'I wanted to go back.'

It's healthier to make a choice because you *want* to do something, than because you *have* to do something. It's empowering – you're in control and you have positive reasons to return.

'I had no choice – I had *to go back.'*

If you feel forced into the 'no choice' corner, it will be harder to think positively about your situation and that will impact on the way you approach people. Your manner, attitude and body language won't encourage potential employers to recruit you; they want to take *you* on, not your baggage. Focus on the positives of returning to work: the fun side, the fact there are so many careers to choose from, the money, friendship, the fact you're needed. If you think you have no choice, you're more likely to waste time and energy contemplating your situation instead of changing things for the better. Concentrate, too, on the choices ahead. You're in the driving seat, and can steer your life in the direction you want to go.

> Make this your journey off to a new start. If you take excess baggage with you, make sure it contains only the good stuff and leave the rest at home!

Let's look at some of the choices you have ahead.

What's motivating your comeback?

You'll have your own reasons for your return. Be clear in your own mind what they are, and it will help you to clarify what you want to get out of your next move.

Case Study: Eric, returning to work

'After my wife died, I didn't really need to work but I felt lost without the routine and companionship. The work I'm doing isn't demanding on my brain, but that's not important. I like the fact that I feel needed, I'm part of a team; there's a social side to the job, too. I love dealing with the customers, and I think many of them welcome a more mature face. A lot of my work colleagues and I are similar in age, and we get together for social outings, which is a real bonus.'

How strongly do the reasons below feature in your plans to go back to work? What's in the return for you and what do you want to get out of it? Rank the following as they feature in importance for you in your return to the workplace.

	Very highly	Highly	Average	Not much
Money – I need to earn £ ___ a month				
For the challenge				
To meet new people				
To have more of a social life				
To get out of this house!				
The kids have all started school – it seems like the logical thing to do				
To be creative				
To run my own business				
To have some fun				
To be seen as me in my own right				
To meet someone special				
To get some independence				
To do something for me				
The Job Centre is hassling me				
I need the routine of work				
To contribute my skills, abilities, talents, experience, passions				
To fulfil a passion				

What does that tell you about your return? Is work the only way to fulfil those things which rank very highly or highly? Are there any other options you should be considering, such as studying, getting involved in voluntary work or taking up a new hobby or interest which would meet your needs and wants? Or does a return to work fit the bill nicely?

Do you want a job or a career?

Depending on what you want out of life and what's motivating you to return to work, you may simply be after a job, or you may want to pursue a career. There's a difference between the two.

The job

- Something to be done, executed, undertaken, such as jobs you'd do at home or in the garden;
- The work – you turn up, do what's required, and then go home. You may do it for the extra income, companionship, to pay the bills, or to get you out of the house.
- A short term thing, although some people can be in a job for years, but that doesn't encompass the idea of a journey, progression and ambition as the term 'career' does.

A university student may have several jobs while studying, but, with thought and careful marketing, these roles can play an important selling point when it comes to securing that first career break.

Work may not be the most important thing in the life of someone who just wants a job, but even so, they have a right to work that they enjoy and are interested in. There's no point in wasting your time and life on something which turns you off.

The career

A career may have some or all of the following characteristics:

- long-term commitment and nurturing;
- constant increase in new responsibilities to take you to the next level;
- working for a professional qualification;
- being a member of a professional body or networking group;
- a long term phenomenon, built on a series of stepping stones over a period of time.

Careers need love and work if they're to develop

Of course, carefully nurtured and tended, a job can turn into a career. Careers need attention, care, work, effort, persistence, motivation and thought, and planning if they are to be rewarding and exciting. A career that doesn't receive regular care, attention and planning from its owner can rapidly turn into 'just a job' and result in dissatisfaction in life overall.

Watch your language!

The language we place on the use of 'job' or 'career' tells people a lot about how we view the role work plays in our lives and the approach we take to it. If you tell recruiters you're looking for a new career, a career shift, a career change, career planning advice, career promotion, then that sends a certain message. If you want to be taken seriously, and want to find a role which will enable you to develop, invest in, reach your potential, challenge you, bring you new skills and capabilities, talk career. Don't talk job.

> The language we use in life affects the way we view ourselves and the way others see us.

Be positive to succeed

Talk success, talk positive, talk about what you want to achieve in life and work, and say 'I will' confidently and you'll succeed. Talk failure, talk negatively, talk about what you don't want and say 'I'll try' – and that's probably what you'll get. You've already given yourself permission and excuses to fail.

Do you plan to live to work or work to live?

Britons have the reputation in Europe for working the longest hours of all, but that doesn't mean you have to follow suit.

How many of the 168 hours you have in a week do you want to be consumed by:

- getting ready for work
- going to work and coming home again
- actually working itself
- being on call
- thinking about work?

We all have our own criteria for this. Most people work 'full time' – say 35–45 hours a week – but that only includes work on its own. Do you want to be so exhausted after work that you have no energy or time for anything else? Or do you want energy and time for activities which are equally important to you, such as socialising, voluntary activities or making love with your partner?

Employers are increasingly prepared to be flexible to keep good staff or to take on staff they want, although smaller ones may find this harder from a practical point of view.

How does work rank with other things which are important to you?

Much will depend on your current situation. Once you know the hours you need or want to work, it will be easier to negotiate with prospective employers.

Acknowledging your essentials

You'll have your own views and values on what you want and need as you proceed with your job search. Consider:

How quickly do you need to find a job?

Even if you urgently need to work for financial reasons, try not to apply for the first job you see. Some thought about what you want to do will mean you are happier and more interested at work. That said, you don't want to still be looking for the right job for you as you breathe your last breath.

How much money do you want or need to make?

Think about your bottom line. How much do you need to earn every month to:

- pay off all the bills
- build up a rainy day fund for your pension, emergencies
- have fun and magic you want in your life, such as holidays and hobbies?
- pay the tax man, your national insurance contributions, your wardrobe, commuter costs – i.e. those working costs which are hidden but compulsory!

Your financial earnings will make a big difference to you and your dependants with regards to the lifestyle you lead. Many companies add perks such as health insurance, pension schemes, performance bonuses, flexitime, gym membership and childcare facilities. If you set up your own business, you may lose these.

A great web site to help you to calculate the basic earnings you'll need is www.ivillage.co.uk/workcareer/cashflow

How much training are you willing to do if you want to change track?

How much training are you prepared to do prior to returning to work? A ten-week course? A year? None at all? Your willingness to train could have a huge impact on the choices ahead of you. It could refresh your skills so you feel more confident and up-to-date returning to work, or enable you to change track completely and move into a new career, or up a gear to a higher level.

What is important to your life style?

Going back to work will change your life.

Think about those things you won't compromise over. We're not as flexible as we like to think we are! Some of the things below may be essential to your life, others may not. Returning to work gives you a great opportunity to review your life overall and make changes for the better.

Exercise 1

Take a sheet of paper and rank the following in order of importance to you:

Time to spend with your partner   _____

Time to spend with your parents/partner's parents   _____

Time with your kids   _____

Time with your pets   _____

Time for friends   _____

Opportunity to travel (not for your job)   _____

A job/career   _____

Your own business   _____

Opportunity to spoil yourself   _____

Taking up something new   _____

Making new friends   _____

Making up for lost education ⎯⎯⎯⎯⎯

Personal development and growth ⎯⎯⎯⎯⎯

Good health ⎯⎯⎯⎯⎯

Exercise and fitness ⎯⎯⎯⎯⎯

Caring for your home and garden ⎯⎯⎯⎯⎯

Assess what each one would mean to you if you achieved it. What would your life be like if you achieved your career goals, or enjoyed that perfect work–life balance, or found great satisfaction in work?

This will help you decide where a job fits into your life. If you had a job you deemed boring for 48 weeks of the year, 40 hours a week, but the rest of your life was fine and dandy, how happy would you be? Would you be pleased with your life as you looked back, or would you wish it had been different?

Exercise 2

Consider:

Which is more important?

Career goals   Work–life balance   Job satisfaction

Picture your life if each item were the most important in your life. Which picture would be the one you want?

Build up a picture

What are the outcomes from Exercises 1 and 2 telling you about the role you want work to play in your life overall?

 ## You're in control

This is your journey back to work, so take time to think and plan carefully:

- What you want to do and achieve.
- Where you want to work – the environment, what sort of workmates you have, etc.
- What you want to get out of work.
- When you want to work.
- How you and your partner will cope with the household chores.

> The more you take control of your own future and know what you want, the more likely you are to get it.

Your attitude counts most

Your life and career are what you make of it. For example, many people do phenomenally well setting up their own businesses, starting out at the kitchen table or in the garden shed or garage, and succeeding beyond their wildest dreams. (Of course, there are also many start ups which fail.) This success may evoke reactions in you such as:

- 'I'd love to do that.'
- 'Oh well, dream on...'
- 'It's all very well for them...'
- 'I wonder how they did it?'
- 'Another person who's made it big. I don't want to make it big. I just want to get out of the house and earn a living so I can enjoy life.'

> You can do it whatever 'it' is.
> You don't have to be an Einstein or Da Vinci to get a job you enjoy.

We all have our own career and life aspirations. What matters is that you know what yours are and that you create the right opportunities to achieve them. This book will help you to make those decisions and hopefully return to work with a lifestyle that suits and delights you.

Do it now

- Write a summary outlining why you want to return to work and what you want to get out of it.
- How much do you belief you deserve this opportunity to change your life?
- What will it mean for you in your own right when you return to work? What will it *do* for you?
- How will your return benefit those you care about in your life?

Summary

Careers and lifestyles are increasingly inter-twined and it's important to get the balance right for you if you're to be happy, healthy and successful.

- Take time to think about how you want your life to look once you return to work.

- *You're* in charge of the process of going back. It is entirely owned and driven by you.

- Be clear about what is essential to you and what you can be flexible about.

2

News From the World of Work

‘Be aware of the choices and you'll make a better choice for you!’

Reflect for a moment on the workplace. Its increasing diversity and rich fabric means more opportunities and a greater choice for you – so you need to assess what you want in order to find the right niche for you. This chapter will help to raise your awareness of the plethora of choices available, and how that has come about, both in terms of what you could do and how you could be employed.

Picturing the workplace

The workplace is like a huge jig-saw consisting of hundreds of pieces. Each different sector forms its own section in that picture, so the overall picture of the puzzle has sections such as:

- Healthcare
- Travel and tourism
- Leisure
- Engineering
- Support staff
- Charity organisations
- Professional and business services
- Creative industries

- Transportation and logistics
- Science
- Personal services
- Security
- Education
- Manufacturing
- Customer services
- Pharmaceuticals
- Human resources and training
- The new technologies
- Information and communications technology
- Land-based industries
- Armed services
- Retail
- Social services
- Marketing and PR
- Building and construction
- Public sector
- Recruitment

Each sector consists of many smaller parts. The health sector, for example, has sections for dentistry, physiotherapy, surgery etc. and each of those has yet more pieces. In dentistry, these include dentists, dental technicians, dental nurses, researchers, dental surgeons, oral surgeons and so on.

Sectors also have their own rules, regulations, patterns of behaviour, approach and organisation. They have their own career paths and rules, and are governed in common by consumer standards and expectations, research and development, international markets and fierce competition, and legislation and regulation. These things all affect your day-to-day experience at work.

Ownership varies, too. Some sectors are state-controlled, others by private individuals, shareholders, stakeholders, you and me. Some are run for profit, others are not. Again, this affects their culture.

The sectors have aspects in common: for example, they are bound by legislation such as health and safety; they are driven by consumer demand and global competition. And those employed in them need transferable skills – that is, skills that will transfer from one piece of the jig-saw to another, such as communication skills, IT and customer service skills. They all need leaders, managers, experts in areas such as human resources, marketing, PR, IT, customer care, administrators, researchers and so on.

So which piece is yours?

The key is to find the bit that suits you the best – somewhere you feel right. Of course, you could add another piece to the jig-saw by starting your own business. You can trust to luck, and pray that you land on the right piece; or you can work out where you want to be.

More careers, new careers

The workplace is expanding all the time, as more niche and specialist areas evolve. Knowledge is a powerful thing and it gives us the opportunity to talk to experts when we buy products and services. We want to talk to people who can advise us, inform us, counsel, facilitate, encourage and recommend. Regulations and legislation have meant that people need to have more expertise in the areas they're working in. Research and development leads to new products, services, ideas and technology, and has transformed the workplace over the centuries, leading to new opportunities and careers. The Internet and communications revolution means that even a one-man band can do business with anyone anywhere in the world. Changes in opportunities and the ways of working, learning and training have enabled you and me to take advantage of these new careers and take more control of the way we work and live.

Each sector has a greater range of jobs available

Science, technology and an increasing emphasis on personal satisfaction, growth and development have resulted in a huge range of new specialist careers. Let's take the pet industry as an example. There are now canine beauticians, pet counsellors, animal therapists and dieticians, animal behaviourists, pet portrait painters, dog walkers and animal aunts. As we acquire more knowledge in this area, there will be more opportunities to specialise.

Changing career paths

Our generations in the twenty first century can enjoy the opportunity to move from one sector to another and so change career in a way our forefathers couldn't, partly because of the numerous opportunities to retrain and to set up a business. Employers too acknowledge that a fresh approach from an outsider to the sector has its benefits; and that since job security is a thing of the past, individuals need to be more open and willing to move to another career.

The instability in the world of employment and the new relationship between employers and employees means that we need to be adept at remaining in work, by having a strong network and excellent work-hunting skills. We will need to be prepared to work for different employers during our lifetime.

I want to change

People are less inclined to spend time in careers they don't enjoy – they want the best in life. There's the 'I can change career and I will,' and then later 'I have – why didn't I do it before?' attitude. Events such as the September 11 terrorist attacks in New York and the tsunami in Asia, or personal events closer to home, such as the death of a family member, remind us how precious life is. They often provide the catalyst for change and the kick up the backside we need to make the change that we need happen.

What does this mean for the individual?

It will be more important than ever for you to have a strong sense of:

- Self-reliance – you must make choices and take full responsibility for the consequences. The more you're able to do this, the more you will get out of life.
- Career and life decision-making skills, as the two become ever more closely linked.
- The importance and willingness to learn new skills and to keep up to date with technology and communications innovations and knowledge.

- Your own worth in the job market.
- Change.
- How to find work and present yourself rapidly to potential employers.
- The opportunities self-employment offers.

You will need these skills, knowledge and resources now even as you start to plot your return to work. This book will help you build them. In short, you need to enhance your employability.

Employability – what does it mean?

The Confederation of British Industries (CBI) describes the term employability briefly as 'simply the ability to be employed.' Figure 1 shows what that means:

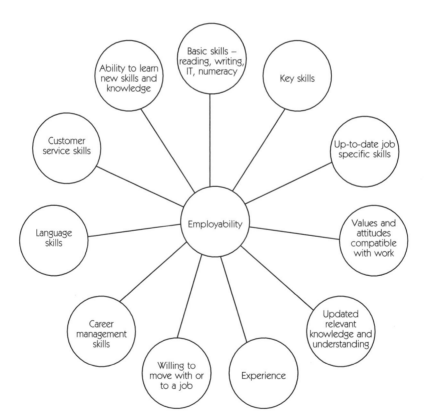

Figure 1. The ability to be employed

To earn a living, a flexible approach to *how* you are employed will be important. You'll need the confidence to consider non-traditional ways of working, such as teleworking, contracting, changing employers if not careers, portfolio working and going freelance to keep the money coming in.

It's never too late

The fact that we all need to enhance our employability means that it's never too late to change career; though some careers have an age ceiling. Many roles strongly benefit from the life experience the more mature individual has to bring.

People change careers for all sorts of reasons: some want greater security, such as the gardener who wants a less physical job as he gets older, or they want to downshift from living in the rat-race to a more relaxed way of life. Many people elect to start a new life abroad, or relocate to the country. Others are forced to re-think, because they have been made redundant or been sacked, or because of their own personal circumstances.

Don't be an 'if only' statistic

Think about the number of times you've heard people say, *I'd love to do something different'* or *'I'd love to run my own business,'* or whatever it is they want to do. I can think of two straightaway, and both worked for a bank. One trained as a commercial pilot, and the other became an air traffic controller. Both fulfilled a dream they'd had. They took the chance, took a risk (it has to be said) and made it work. *They made it happen.* You can, as well.

It's not too late to retrain

One of the oldest people in the UK to get a degree recently was 88 years old! The key is to show that maturity and life experience are assets. Admissions tutors welcome mature students (i.e. those over 21). They are serious about their studies and highly motivated, organised and dedicated, and prepared to make sacrifices to achieve their goals.

There are no excuses *not* to learn. We live in an 'any time, any place' society; you can learn many subjects at your own pace at home, in your public library, your local college or adult education centre, on the Internet, by distance learning or at a college or university. Many professional bodies run refresher courses for people returning to their old career, whilst others offer taster sessions for those contemplating moving to it. If your study skills are rusty, take advantage of the many return to study courses, designed to boost your confidence and study know-how. Recent studies prove to an employer that you're committed to your next career move.

As the world changes, employers need staff who can keep up with change, keep learning and move with the times. Maybe their sector has new regulations that they have to keep up to date with, or new technology, products, developments, research, or discoveries. If you go to your doctor, you like to think she's up to date with all the latest research and new medicines on the market, don't you? Your doctor needs to keep learning to keep up to date. How she does that will depend on how she prefers to learn.

> Qualifications alone aren't enough to secure success in job hunting. Your ability to network, market and sell yourself will be important factors in succeeding too.

Acknowledging different ways of working

You not only have more choice in the career you go for, you can decide *how* you want to work! For example, have you considered these examples:

Portfolio worker – Carl works for two employers: a travel agent in the morning and a nursery in the afternoon.

Full time – Meg works full-time for one employer – she does a 35-hour week.

Part time – Udi works for one employer for 20 hours a week.

Flexitime – Adrian works 10 hours a day for 4 days a week and has Friday off.

Temporary worker – Marge works as and when she wants in theory. In practice she is more flexible that that: her flexibility makes her a more successful 'temp'.

Contract worker – Joel is engaged on a contract for 6 months with a company. After the 6 months are up, the contract may be renewed. If it isn't, Joel knows he needs to look for work elsewhere.

Job share – Marion and David share a full-time job. Marion does mornings, and David does afternoons. Down the corridor from their office, Sandi works Monday, Tuesday and Wednesday morning, while Eli works the rest of the week.

Working a set number of hours a year. Madelene works 1,600 hours a year for her bank. At the start of the year, she and her line-manager work out the busy times when Madelene will need to do the bulk of her 1,600 hours.

Term time only – Adele is a grandmother. She works term time only and has holidays off to look after her grandchildren.

Working for yourself – Natalie has set up her own business.

Network marketing – Steve recruits other people to sell products for him. He manages the business in the mornings and has the afternoons off.

The advantage of this to an employer is clear: he or she can develop a flexible workforce which can respond to customer demands. *Career breaks, retainer schemes and parental leave* all enable employers to offer flexible working patterns to staff who need or wish to take time out. Such flexible ways of working also enable employers to staff their companies for longer periods of time in the day – which is what customers want.

The benefit to you is that it is possible to find the balance you need between work and life, although this will depend on the kind of work you want to do.

Flexibility is nonetheless the key to success

There will always be conflicts to be resolved between the needs of the business and its employees, not just in terms of the customers' demands but also friction between those at work with dependants (be they elderly or young) and those without. Not every company offers flexible working conditions; their web sites and company literature will give you an idea of how far they go. This sort of flexibility is often very difficult for smaller companies where an 'all hands on deck' ethos is crucial for survival. Part-time workers' rights are improving all the time but employers and employees need to work together and be aware of each other's needs. For many individuals, that doesn't give them enough control and so they choose the self-employed route.

Do it now

- Find three people who have changed career. Talk to them about how they did it and what it's done for them.
- How far does the thought of creating your own piece of the jig-saw i.e. setting up your own business, excite you?
- Identify your preferred way of working. How will that fit in with your lifestyle needs you decided were important to you in Chapter 1?

 ## Summary

The world is constantly changing, so the workplace and the opportunities within it must also keep changing.

- Recognise that you need to keep learning to stay on top of the sector you decide to work in.

- Think of your career as being like your skin: you constantly need to renew it to keep it fresh and alive.

- The opportunity to change career and find a working pattern to suit you is greater now than it has ever been before.

3

So What's Your Game Plan?

‘Have a goal to aim for and you'll focus less on the obstacles.’

Now that you've established why you want to return to work, this chapter is designed to help you to take control of your move back to work. It will help you see a path back to work, so that you know what you need to do and when to do it. This will boost your feelings of control and make the whole thing more manageable. One way to do this is to set yourself a goal to achieve.

Setting goals

Those people who have a goal find that they focus more on the end result – in your case, a return to work – and less on the obstacles and barriers in front of them. Goals boost your chances of success: you can clearly see what you want to achieve and when you want to achieve it by. Visualising success enhances your chances of achieving it.

Make your goal happen for you! Now!

You're far more likely to achieve your goal of returning to work if it is:

- **Personal to you**, so that you understand the importance of achieving it.
- **Visual in your mind**. Build a picture around your goals. What will your life be like when you've gone back to work?
- **Written down**. Goals that aren't written down lose their impact. Write your goal down and put it somewhere you can see it regularly. For example, *I will be back at work by September 2006.*
- **In the present tense**. Start behaving and talking to yourself as if you are already doing what you want to do. For example, devote the same number of hours to your return to work as you propose to give to working.
- **Positive**. Talk about what you *do* want to do as opposed to what you don't. Make notes as thoughts occur to you in a file or notebook to build up a picture of what you want to do.
- **Specific**. It will help you focus.
- **Challenging**. If your goal is too easy to achieve, you'll get bored. If it's unachievable, you'll get despondent. Give yourself a goal which stretches you and that you enjoy working towards.
- **Given a time limit**. Presumably, you want to go back to work in the next few weeks, months or year. Or is your time limit without an end, in which case you'll be less focused on achieving it?

You could draw yourself a time-line, as the example in Figure 2 shows, to give yourself an idea of what you need to do.

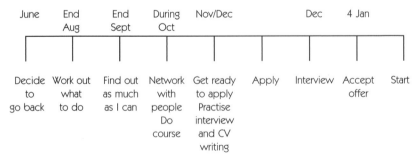

Figure 2. A time-line.

Talk to those closest to you

If you've got a partner and/or children, you may want to take them on board when putting your goal together, particularly if they will be affected, as John's wife Susanne was:

Example: John sets his goal

John wanted to go back to work after six months' out looking after his wife following a road accident. He didn't want to rush it because he wanted to make sure his wife could cope first. His goal, which he worked out with his wife, was:

> 'I will return to work at my company in July 2004 in a similar role that I was in before, and will contact my supervisor to make sure this happens. Susanne and I will start living day to day as if I was at the office so that we can start identifying possible problems which may occur. The benefits of going back are: Susanne knows she is well enough for me to go back; we'll have my full salary back; I'll be glad to be back with my colleagues doing work I find challenging and interesting.'

You'll see from John's goal that:

- He has given it a time scale – July 2004 – so that he and Susanne have something to aim for.
- He and his wife have decided together how to manage John's return, visualising success to such an extent that they start living as if he were already back.
- They are both looking for the benefits of that goal and so focusing on the positive.
- The goal is personal to them, taking into account their current circumstances.

Once you've got your goal, break it down into manageable steps

Goals boost your confidence and give you something to focus on, but they can seem huge, so it can help to break them down into manageable parts:

In John's case, this meant:

1. Identifying the date when he wanted to return;

2. Working out how he and his wife were going to prepare for his return;

3. Contacting his manager to discuss his return; this could mean options such as:
   - could John go into the office for key meetings and work from home initially?
   - could he increase that time to 50% in the office and part time at home?
   - could he change his role?
   - would his role have changed anyway in his absence?
   - looking for projects John could get his teeth into so that he can get back to work gradually.

4. Doing what was necessary to ensure that Susanne had the support she needed at home during the day and talking to any third parties to secure that support, such as district nurses.

5. Finding out what support either John or Susanne's families could offer them.

John kept his employer on his side by being honest and open about his needs, being flexible in terms of the role he took on when he went back, and asking for work he could do from home.

How far ahead do you want to look?

For some people, getting a job at all in the next 6 months will be their goal and feel like a huge achievement, while others take a longer-term view and look five or ten years down the line. Build a goal you feel comfortable with, which is within your reach. If you have been out of work for a long time due to illness, and your doctor is advising a slow, steady return to work, balance your health with your career goals so that they don't cancel each other out.

Achieving your goal

If you have a specific goal, you can get far more done in a much shorter time-scale because you don't waste any time deviating from your route. The five stages in Figure 3 (pp. 28, 29) outline a route to achieving a career goal.

The importance of 'I will'

Many people don't achieve their goals because they are only committed to 'trying' to achieve them. Trying and doing are two different things. The moment you say that you'll 'try' to do something, you've admitted to yourself that you're not whole-heartedly committed to doing it. You're already creating an avenue for escape, or preparing yourself for failure. Banish the word 'try' from your vocabulary. Replace it with the words 'will' or 'do'. Use strong action words, not promises.

> Do something towards your goal to return to work
> every single day – however small.
> Every action you take will move you closer to your return to work.

Exterminating your gremlins!

At this stage, dump any gremlins in your closet which could hinder your chances of achieving your goal. Strengthen your belief in yourself.

Banish negative thoughts and habits you've picked up

Once you've got into the habit of thinking negatively, you need to make a conscious effort to get out of it. Challenge every single negative thing you say about yourself, such as:

Stage 1
What do you want to achieve in 1, 5, 10 or 15 years' time?

Chapters 1–8 will help you here.

What do you want to achieve in your working life? This will involve considering questions such as:

- What do you care about? What excites and interests you?
- What do you want to achieve at work?
- What are your strengths and talents?
- What motivates you?
- Who do you want to work for?
- Do you want to work for yourself?
- Do you want to go back to what you were doing?
- What sort of people do you want to serve?
- What do you and your family need once you've gone back to work?
- What will the benefits be to you and your family?
- What will success mean to you?

Stage 2
What needs to happen for you to achieve this?

Chapters 9–15 will help you work this out.

What do you need to do to make your vision happen? What do you need to start doing? This will mean considering things such as:

- Training and learning to give you the skills and knowledge you need.
- Crash courses.
- Refresher courses.
- Work experience.
- Voluntary work.
- Inner resources, such as motivation, confidence, self-belief, the ability to tackle and overcome barriers which may get in the way of your success.
- Talk to your employer if you're still with them but on a career break or sick leave.

Figure 3: Achieving a career goal

Stage 3
What options are there and what is best for you?

Again, Chapters 9–15 will ask you the questions you need to answer.

This is where you can consider things such as:

- What are all the different ways to achieve the return to work you want?
- How quickly do you want to return to work?
- How best do you learn?
- How do your career plans fit in with your family's needs and your lifestyle wishes?
- How are you going to fund any training or business you want to set up?
- Your character and personality – some people are better suited to self-employment than others, for example.

Stage 4
What are you going to do and when are you going to do it?

Working through the book will help you take the actions you need to help you achieve your goal.

Identify everything you need to do to make your career goal happen and work out what you're going to do and when. Examples are:

- Writing a CV
- Applying for work
- Interviewing
- Setting up your own business
- Networking
- Taking any relevant training you need
- Updating your skills and knowledge
- Boosting your confidence through voluntary work or work experience
- Talking to your line-manager or human resources if you plan to return to the same organisation

Stage 5
Enjoying the change and setting your next goal.

Chapters 16–18 will help you celebrate and move on.

Going back to work will be a big change in your life, so work out some strategies to ensure you manage it brilliantly. Once you've settled down, you can start plotting your next move!

Criticising yourself

I'm hopeless at...   *How do you know?*
I'm not much good at...   *What evidence have you got that*
                                      you're hopeless?
                                      How often have you tried to...?

Limiting beliefs about your abilities

I was useless at school, so why   *So maybe the school environment*
should I be any different now?   *wasn't right, or you didn't like the*
                                      the teacher, or you mucked about...
Oh, I could never do that!   *Have you tried it?*

Saying

I'll try...   *I will...*

Giving yourself excuses for failing before you start...

I'm really busy but I'll try to   *If it's really important to you,*
fit it in...   *you'll make time.*

Not giving your goal the prominence in your life that it deserves

Just one more episode of   *Self care and relaxation is*
Coronation Street and a glass   *important but you need to set up a*
of wine, and I'll get started   *system of rewards for a job well*
                                      done. Be disciplined.

Listening to generalisations from people who don't know what they're talking about

Oh you're too old to change   *So they're career experts now,*
career!   *are they?*

Moaning about your current situation instead of doing something about it

I'd love to, but...

What would your life be like if you did change the situation for the better ... What's stopping you?

Wasting time thinking

What if...?
If only...

How much time are you going to waste thinking?

Blaming someone or something else

Of course, employers never look at anyone over the age of 35 any more...

Where's your evidence?
How many people do you know who are employed over 35?
How will blaming someone else change the situation to bring you the result you want?

You can choose to believe whether you're hopeless or not at something. The next time you find yourself thinking negatively about something, challenge yourself!

- Ask yourself where the evidence is that you're hopeless or can't do something. Have you ever tried it? How do you know? Has someone told you you're hopeless? How do they know?
- Replace your negative thoughts with positive ones. *I'm hopeless at meeting people* can turn into *but I'm a great listener, and people like that.*

You won't kick the habit in a couple of goes. If you've been telling yourself you're hopeless for years, you've got some work to do. Negative thoughts waste your time and energy. You don't need them anymore, so dump them – fast!

Don't procrastinate!

People often procrastinate because they fear failure and so they tell themselves – logically – *Well, if I don't do anything, I won't fail.* So:

- Set yourself a given period of time to do something, e.g. by the end of the week, you will have contacted local colleges or visited a web site for information.
- Challenge your fears: what's the worst that could happen if things go wrong?
- Set yourself daily targets: *I'll make that call before the kids get home from school, while the house is quiet.*
- Break down your action plan into small stages.

Boosting your confidence

Remind yourself of something you're good at straight away and give yourself the evidence that you are! You can't dispute evidence. Get your friends and family to help you. (If you have one person who is continually negative about you, don't involve them.) Pin your list up where you can see it. Recognise your potential and yourself for what you truly are – a fantastic unique individual!

Go out of your comfort zone

When you start heading out into the job market, it can feel very uncomfortable. Get used to it now by practising putting yourself *outside* that place where you feel safe and know what you're doing i.e. your comfort zone. If you stay in your own world, it will be much harder to adapt to the rapidly changing world around you, so get out there and get used to feeling uncomfortable. You'll be amazed at how well you cope.

So jolt yourself out of your usual routine and do something different. Here are some ideas:

- Attend an adult education course to re-boot your brain and learn a new skill.
- Ask a friend to give you a mock interview.
- Make a speech in public.
- Do something absolutely wacky you've always wanted to do but haven't dared to do yet.
- Try a totally new hairstyle or dress code.
- Revamp your day-to-day routine.
- Cook something new.
- Ask someone you fancy on a date.
- Ask someone you don't know well if they'd like to go for a coffee – will you find a new friend?
- Do some voluntary work for a charity you've always wanted to help out.
- Get some work experience in your dream job (or one close to it!).

> **The more you do, the more you will want to do**
> **And the more you *know* you can do.**

It's a great way to meet new people (and expand your network) and boost your confidence to handle new situations, including to meet others who've done just what you're heading out to do.

Assessing your assets

Say the word 'assets' and most people think immediately about money, bank accounts, investment portfolios and so on. However, this is about *your* assets – your skills, achievements, inner strengths, knowledge and networks you have. For example, if you have raised children, you have considerable knowledge about that subject. You may have tremendous juggling skills, as you handle your toddler pulling at your jeans, loading washing in the machine, answering the phone and stopping the dog eating supper. It's easy to forget how skilled and knowledgeable you truly are, so keep listing all those things you can do and know about. One particular skill, combined with knowledge you already have, could just point you in the direction of your next career.

You are an outstanding individual with unique qualities and talents. You have within you incredible passion, self-belief, confidence, capabilities and aspirations. If you're reading this and thinking, *Well, that doesn't sound like me* that's because no one has ever told you so before.

Case Study: Freddie, started own business

'I'd always had a flair for fashion and instinctively knowing what suited my friends and family – they frequently came to me for help in finding suitable outfits for special occasions. When I went back to work, I thought seriously about what I was interested in and had a talent for. By testing my abilities on friends of friends, I discovered I had a real opportunity to set myself up as an image consultant and personal shopper. My 'testers' gave me lots of positive feedback, which gave me lots of confidence. Zone in on what you're good at in life – that will help point you in the right direction.'

> Make your knowledge, achievements and skills come alive for you.
> Remind yourself you've got them.
> Ask yourself what motivated you to get them.

Make your maturity an asset

Increasing numbers of employers welcome mature people back with open arms, such as ASDA and B&Q. Many want to show a family-friendly and all-age face, and seek people who are that bit older who have experience of life and can empathise with people from a wider spread of backgrounds, who have faced the problems and challenges life brings. And many are ideal for people who have done something else in life first, and offer tremendous purpose and satisfaction to those working in them. Examples are:

- Financial advice services
- Careers services
- Retail
- Hotel management
- Local government
- Charities

- Introductory agencies
- House-sitting
- Teaching
- Training
- Museums
- Insurance
- Health care
- Probation service
- Social services
- Working with children
- Public relations
- Teaching English
- The church
- Animal care
- Funeral services
- Customer care
- Media
- Police services
- Management
- Working with the elderly
- Life coaching
- Journalism

Remember that these are just examples and not an exclusive list.

There is no point whinging about people over 40 or 50 not being wanted by employers. It won't get you anywhere, and it certainly won't land you a job. The key is to find out what sectors *are* taking on the mature worker and which companies *do* favour them and target those. Visit web sites such as *www.maturityworks.co.uk* which have advice for the older worker. Consider starting up your own business or buying a franchise or freelancing.

Late entry advice

Many professional bodies have information for you if you're considering a change of career; and if you consult the book *Occupations* in any careers or reference library, you'll find a section 'Late entry' under each occupation with guidelines for the non-school leaver.

Enlisting a careers expert

You can use the Internet and printed material to help you access the mine of information available on careers, education, training and self-employment. But it's also good to talk things through with someone, and the problem with friends and family is that they'll have their own agendas to consider. Enter the impartial careers expert.

Taking on a careers counsellor/coach

What's the difference?

A *careers counsellor* will help you assess your capabilities and skills, strengths and weaknesses, your interests and aspirations and help you match those to opportunities in the workplace.

A *careers coach* helps you identify how you're going to cross the gap between where you are now and where you want to be.

A *careers adviser* will recommend that you take a particular course of action.

Some careers experts combine all three roles, first helping you decide what you want to do, then what you need to do to make that happen; and finally recommending a course of action for you to take. They may advise you on your CV and check it for you, and give you interview practice and mock psychometric tests.

Careers experts work in job centres, schools, colleges, private enterprises, self-employment, probation services, the armed services and other organisations. Your *Yellow Pages* will have details. Make sure your careers expert is trained, qualified and experienced, and find out what and if they charge in advance of starting any sessions.

Finally, careers personnel are not magicians. It is up to you to put the effort in if you are to obtain the results you want – success will require persistent motivation and effort on your part.

Do it now

- Write down your goal to return to work.
- Add how much that goal has empowered you.
- Pin it up somewhere you can see it.
- Reaffirm it to yourself every single day.
- Start using the words 'I will...' instead of 'I will try to...'.

Summary

Clearly defined goals which mean something to us and endorse the values we hold dear will motivate us more than simply making vague statements.

- You can set goals in any area of your life – career, health, finance, fitness.

- We need to ensure that the language we use is going to boost our chances of success, not limit them.

- The more we do, the more we know we can do; but we have to push ourselves outside the boundary we give ourselves to make this belief real.

4

So What Next?

The great thing in this world is not so much where we are, but in what direction we are moving.

Oliver Wendell Holmes

The next three chapters will help you assess whether you are ready for a total change with lots of exercises to do. The only right answers are honest ones; they provide a great chance for you to start building up evidence of the skills and capabilities you have. Even if you're convinced that going back to what you knew is right for you, take time to do them. You could be surprised!

Assessing yourself is a must!

Self-assessment is a vital part of career planning, but often the most overlooked. Many of us find it hard to think about our strengths, talents, values and needs – especially if we're used to putting the needs of others first.

Case study: Angela, now a financial adviser

The hardest bit for me was sitting down after all these years of looking after a family and trying to concentrate on my needs and what I wanted. It was terribly difficult at first to focus and it certainly took a bit of practice, but thinking about my skills, projects and interests helped me think about what I'm good at and enjoy.

Learn to assess yourself with confidence!

As a result of assessing yourself, you will:

1. Have a better idea of what you want to do.
2. Gain self-confidence and boost your belief in your abilities.
3. Be able to deal with possible attempts by family and friends to put you off track.
4. Know exactly what information you need to plan your career.
5. Be able to develop the skills you want to use at work.
6. Know where your weaknesses are and identify gaps in your knowledge and skills so that you can tackle them.
7. Go into any selection situation with a real sense of pride and achievement.
8. Be able to show a potential employer what you can do for them.
9. Be able to talk about your achievements and abilities in interview and sell yourself to an employer.
10. Learn something about yourself that you never knew before, or that you did know, but you'd forgotten.

Going back or moving on?

What could you do next? Here are some of your options:

1. Going back to the same employer in a similar role – you may have been on a career break or sabbatical and have an agreement with your company to go back.
2. Asking your last employer if they will have you back – you left them before your break.
3. Doing what you did before but for a new employer, perhaps even in a new sector.

4. Shifting career, for example, focusing on training and coaching if you were a manager before and those skills formed a part of your role.

5. Doing contract or temporary assignments for a time to see how you feel once you go back.

6. Going freelance and offering your skills, knowledge and expertise for a fee, for example, per hour or per piece of work.

7. Starting your own business, either in something completely new or using the same skills and knowledge that you used before.

8. Changing career altogether.

9. Moving to lower or higher level roles, depending on what you want from work.

10. Getting any job to keep the cash coming in while you think about it.

11. Being an interim manager.

12. Forgetting the whole thing altogether and taking off again to travel, study, to do voluntary work.

13. Signing up as unemployed and doing nothing.

14. Turning your past break to your advantage by turning whatever it was that you were doing during the break into a career.

15. Working in a new location, such as abroad or in another part of the country.

These choices are probably open to you whether you're choosing to go back or you feel you 'have' to go back.

 ## Returning to what you know

Going back to what you knew before may seem like a short cut route to get back into paid employment, especially if you managed to keep up a strong network of contacts and you excelled at what you did. But ask yourself how different things will be there when you return, and how much *you've* changed in the time you've been taking a break.

Assess the state of the sector you were in

Case Study: Jan, returning from 9 months' travel

'I came back from an exhilarating nine months' travelling and intended to go straight back into a similar role I'd had before I left. Unfortunately, while I'd been away, the job market had changed and nobody was recruiting. Eventually, I went freelance and got some work through old colleagues. Three years later, I'm still freelancing and much preferring my current lifestyle to the old one I had. I'm also getting more money than I did before. You've just got to be flexible and think about what your customers want and how you can fill any gaps.'

Checklist

What is the job market like in your sector? Where are the opportunities?   _____

What can you do to update yourself with new developments and products, technology and trends?   _____

Will you need to diversify to strengthen your chances of securing work?   _____

Will you need to look at getting work in a different way?   _____

How will you need to change your strategy to find work to ensure success?   _____

How can you sell the skills you've acquired during your break from employment so that they will clearly benefit employers who recruit you?   _____

Can you find a mentor to help you make your return happen?   _____

How will you need to update your skills and knowledge so that you can hit the ground running?   _____

What returner schemes are available for people like yourself who have had a break?   _____

Have recruitment methods changed, and if so, how?   _____

Contact professional organisations relevant to your sector to find network groups in your area for help and support. The web site *www.worktrain.gov.uk* has a huge number of links to professional bodies, or you can find yours through *Occupations,* available in any careers library, or surfing the Net. These may cover issues such as training, career development, what's hot, new products and services, and so on. The web sites of professional bodies will have details of any networking groups in your area. If there is no group, why not start one up on your own? Write an article for the local paper, or put an ad in it, or put up a web page to hook interest. Keep in touch with new contacts you make – don't let those business cards gather dust in a drawer. Keep them alive and active.

What's happened to your employer?

If you're thinking of going back to the role you once had with the same organisation, questions to ask are:

Does your previous job still exist?   _____
What has changed in the organisation?   _____
Does the company still exist? Has it merged with or been
taken over by another?   _____
If the answer to either of these first questions is no,
what has replaced it/them?   _____
Would you want the same level of responsibility
you had before?   _____
Have your views on what constitutes the perfect role for you
changed in the time you've been out of the workplace?   _____
Would you regret the chance you now have to try something
new if you went back to the same thing?   _____

Yes, you're definitely going back...

If you've had to take some time out, try to keep in touch with the organisation by:

- Emailing colleagues to find out what's happening.
- Meeting a couple of times with your line-manager.
- Attending team meetings if you can.

- Dropping in for a coffee or meeting a close colleague or your line-manager for lunch.
- Receiving up dates from your employer.
- Showing an interest in what is happening.
- Going in to visit.
- Learning about new products and services which are available.

Take yourself forward 40 years and look back at your life. Would you then regret it if you didn't take the opportunity you have now to do something different?

Organisations move on, with or without you!

Even if you've only had a short break from the workplace, things will have changed, so talk to people in the field and spend a couple of days with them to find out what's different. Ask yourself:

- What's everyone talking about and excited by?
- What are they finding challenging and frustrating?
- Are working conditions still the same?
- What new products or services are they working with?
- How has technology impacted on the working day? Is the routine still the same?

Read trade and professional magazines (your newsagent or a good reference library will have these), journals and books. Be able to talk about what's going on and show that you're very much interested in it. You need to prove this to yourself as much as to any potential employer.

You've changed too!

You're not the same person going back to work that you were when you left it. Your experiences since being in work will have changed your attitude and outlook on life in some way. How do you respond to what you see, hear and feel around you? Are you excited, passionate and ready to shoot back? Or are you left thinking, *'Oh this old job again. All the familiar faces and problems. I guess it will pay the bills...'*.

Be prepared to let go

You may be dismayed to find that you're uninspired by what you see, and experience panic that a return to what you knew won't work. Build on all the skills and experience you've acquired in your life thus far overall, and be ready to let go. You deserve better than second best.

Look to learn from your past working life. What behaviour and approaches led to success? What sort of working environment did you thrive in and feel happiest in? Which ingredients of all the different roles you held did you love the most? If there are very few you can remember with excitement and passion, move on to a role you know you'll love and get stuck into!

Shifting career

You could shift career, which means staying in the same sector and taking one part of your role and expanding it considerably so that it becomes a full time one.

You would still use the same skills, interests and abilities in the new career as you did in your old one. A nurse might change her career to become a counsellor or work for a health promotion unit, teach student nurses or enter management, personnel or sales. These careers demand skills in communicating with a wide variety of people, often under pressure and in sensitive situations. The post-holders must be able to gain the confidence of others, to advise their customers and to share information with them in a way in which they will understand. They require the ability to pay close attention to detail, an insight into human nature, and the ability to keep records. They call for patience, tact and tenacity. They also cater for people who have a strong interest in health, psychology and helping others.

Case study: Gary, Web Designer

'I was working in a large organisation doing presentations before I took time out. When I planned my return, I realised I wanted to do some designing, because I love being creative. I still do presentations if I'm asked, but as part of my own business in which I also design web sites. Both arms of my business means I can spread my chances of being in work. I couldn't see myself going back to work for someone else, so setting up on my own has been ideal. I choose my own hours, my own clients – and make the most of my creative talents.'

Equally you could move sideways

Sideways moves are great if you want to go back to the same organisation but the slot you were originally in has been deleted due to restructuring, or someone else has taken it over. Sideways shifts enable you to start afresh for the same company, but you can also take a different slant. If your organisation offers that to you, don't turn it down. Consider it, and if you take it up, work to make sure it works out for you.

Re-inventing your career

A career change may be just what you need – a chance to start afresh. Remember, skills transfer. Plenty of the skills you used in your previous career will be relevant in your new one, such as communication skills, handling difficult people, problem solving, team working, numeracy and information technology. You'll probably need to learn new skills and knowledge if you're starting another career, but there are plenty of opportunities to do that. Equally, you could turn a hobby into a money making enterprise.

Let's look at some aspects to consider if you want a fresh start.

How much responsibility do you want this time?

There are pros and cons to having responsibility such as:

Low	*High*
Less money	More money
In and out, no need to think about work after you've left it for the day	You could take it home with you – literally or in your thoughts and mind
Day-to-day view of work	Tendency to think longer term re your career, the organisation, the people working for you
You manage yourself, your work, your time	You manage others and yourself
More routine	Less routine
Less say in the direction of the company	More say in the direction of the company
More contact with customers	Less contact with customers – you have to stand back from the day-to-day stuff and think about the future

Here are two lists of jobs, each paired off. Compare the level of responsibility they have and how that impacts on the work they do and their lives outside of work.

Nurse	Doctor
Teacher	Head teacher
Probation officer	Social worker
Waitress	Hotel manager
Retail manager	Chief executive of retail company
Film editor	Film director
Web designer	Entrepreneur

Think about yourself

Which level of responsibility appeals to you and excites you more? The more you have, the more that may overlap into other areas of your life. Of course you may enjoy the responsibility so much that you don't care about that. Much depends on what you want to achieve at work: if you want to change the way something is done and influence the health of others, for example, that's a big responsibility. If you want 'a job' then you're more likely to limit and put boundaries on your levels of responsibility and accountability.

What are your ambitions?

Do you want to be able to look back at the end of your working life and say, *'My business did well. I set it up and succeeded!'* or to know that you got to the top in the corporate world? Do you want to enjoy the successes (monetary and otherwise) or handle the failures yourself? Do you want to create the vision for a business and see it through to fruition, or be part of an organisation which strives to achieve a particular vision, however senior you are in that. Do you want to be a small team that drives a business forward? Or do you want to look back and know that you enjoyed work, but it didn't rule your life?

What will you tolerate and what will frustrate you?

Do you dislike being hemmed in by procedures, regulations and conformity? Or do you find those comforting and fear creativity, independence and freedom? There are more regulations and legislation now than ever before for businesses to adhere to. Looking back at your career, what environment did you thrive best in; what tolerated and frustrated you and what would you like to be clear of next time round?

What will fit into your life?

Now that you've been out of work for a break, how do you feel about going back to the routine of working life? Are you looking forward to it and have you thought seriously about how it will affect your daily life, and that of your family?

Case study: Mark contemplating his return

Mark has been a househusband for three years while his wife Adele worked. John is now ready to go back to work, as their three children will be in nursery or school next September, but he says: 'I'm going to work for myself. After the freedom I've enjoyed of being able to set pretty much my own hours, I don't think I could work for anyone else now. I want that flexibility.'

We all have our own needs in life and you need to consider how the different ways of being employed will affect your lifestyle and finances. For example:

- How would you cope financially if you had no regular salary, and the perks you'd previously received from past employers (pension, private health insurance, bonuses, shares, free gym membership, flexitime, medical check ups...) were no longer part of the package?
- How will you look after elderly relatives and children while you're working for another employer? What will you do if you're working on an order on which your business is dependent and one of your kids falls sick?
- Do you prefer to work in a team of people or are you very self-motivated and driven to succeed on your own? Can you survive without the companionship of colleagues at work, even if they are all spread out over a number of locations?

What are your values?

Your return to work will enable you to re-align your values – those ideals, behaviour, passions you hold most dear in life – with your next career move. For example, if the ability to be creative is important to you, careers which allow yours to blossom will be along the right lines. Careers in more formal structured organisations may dent your creativity and leave you feeling frustrated.

We all have different values. The following are examples.

Achievement	Integrity	Dependability
Creativity	Co-operation	Ambition
Honesty	Excellent performance	Caring
Making a difference	Success	Happiness
Wealthy	Independence	Work–life balance
Contribution	Education	Work
Fun	Love	Healthy
Fitness	Considerate	Hospitable
Welcoming	Results-oriented	Sense of humour
Passionate	Non-judgemental	Kind
Lover of life	Social	Artistic
Freedom	Looking forward	Staying put
Time for what's important	Status	Respect
	Choice	

1. List those which are most important to you at work.

2. Now write a specific description of each one of your important values. We all have our definitions of, say, 'integrity' or 'independence'. In particular, people's definition of 'wealth', 'happiness' and 'success' are – well, each very much to their own. Write down *your* definition – that's the one that matters.

3. Do this exercise with a friend and compare notes. How do your answers differ?

4. How far do you feature these values in your life right now? How far did your last career reflect and encompass them?

5. How could they be incorporated in your future working life? For example, if you wanted to make a difference, be specific about how, to whom, what you want to do, when you want to do it. Chapters 5 and 6 will help you build on this.

6. What are your thoughts or values telling you about yourself and your future?

7. What conclusions do you draw about your next career role?

Take your time, if you can

A break from work provides a good opportunity to re-charge your batteries and discover some of the creativity within you that living life often stamps out. Use that break – don't waste it.

Do it now

- Look at a decision you've made recently. How did you approach it?
- What could you do differently next time that would make your decision-making skills more effective?
- How often do you let the views of others influence your actions? When was the last time this happened?
- What can you do to change this situation?

Summary

Be sure in your own values and beliefs: do you want to go back to what you knew, or start again to do something fresh?

- Even if you think you want to return to the same role you were in before, assess yourself and what you want. You could discover that you want a totally new direction!

- You can change, shift, tweak or remain in your career – that's up to you.

- Don't limit yourself to thinking about working for others. If you're a budding entrepreneur, you could work for yourself.

5

What's Your Dream Job?

6Choose a job you love, and you will never work a day again in your life.9

Confucius

When you're telling people that you plan to return to work and they ask you what you're going to do, what's your reaction? Do you know or do you feel like a lot of folk when faced with such a question and your mind goes blank? Many people hit a brick wall when considering what they want to do at work, which is often why they choose the first thing they see. This chapter will help you disassemble the bricks of that wall and give you a clear indication of what you want to do.

And why aren't you doing it?

So what's your dream job and why aren't you doing it? There are many reasons why people don't follow their dream job – perhaps they see it as just that, a dream. But dreams can turn into reality so if you once had a dream career, re-visit and research it. What stopped you following your dream job before? Were you afraid that someone would laugh at you? Were you expected to be something respectable? Or did you think you could never achieve it?

Life is not a dress rehearsal – this is it!

This is your time to work out what you want to do in future that will fulfil *you* and bring *you* enjoyment and satisfaction. It is the perfect time to analyse your life and identify what you want to do more of, what you want to get rid of, by delegating it or eliminating the task altogether and what you want to introduce into it.

Taking action on passions

When you think of work, the words passion, excitement, love, purpose and contribution don't exactly spring to mind. Yet imagine if you woke up every morning passionate and excited about the day ahead, what would your life be like? As people go through life and realise how precious it is, many of us start to take far more seriously our purpose and contribution on this earth. Imagine if you discovered the contribution you really wanted to make at work, what would life be like for you then?

Consider the following

If you were to look forward to your retirement years, or even writing your epitaph, what would you want to be looking back on? Use these questions to help write your own epitaph now:

- What successes would feature in your life?
- What impact would you have made on humanity, or the earth?
- What difference would you have made and who would it have had an impact on?
- What do you really care about? What would make you leap out of bed on a cold, wet, dark morning?
- What did you do *anything* for?
- What voluntary work did you participate in? What appealed to you about it?
- If you'd won the Lottery, what would you have done?

Build up a picture of the difference you want to make in your life before you retire, and you'll be in a better position to find work you love which really means something to you.

There are more opportunities to follow passion now

A whole host of careers has grown up around passions and things which are important to us. Who would have thought that the sports sector would be the way it is now? There are a huge number of careers related to sports and all those employing people in clubs, organisations and societies. Similarly, there are hundreds of charities, all working to make a difference to those they serve and employing people in various roles. So if you want to make a difference to your passion, you could:

1. Do nothing at all.
2. Follow it from the sidelines.
3. Get actively involved as a volunteer.
4. Work for an organisation right in it.

Charities frequently offer great perks, flexible working patterns and the opportunity to develop a good work–life balance. And when you leave work at the end of the day, you know you've really made a difference.

Being a social entrepreneur

Social entrepreneurs start up businesses or organisations for the benefit of the community or those who need help, or to promote a particular theme, such as healthy living. Social entrepreneurship enables you to make a difference and make a living. Social enterprises use business techniques to achieve social aims, such as job creation, training, housing trusts. The community benefits from any financial surplus, rather than shareholders and owners. They may take the form of housing trusts and co-operatives. See Useful Addresses for more information.

When you were 5...

The child in us is a wonderful thing. It's curious, inquisitive and questioning. Unfortunately, the child tends to get buried under mortgages, tax returns, nappies, car insurance, the middle-age bulge and droop and exhaustion.

Exercise

Go somewhere quiet. Shut your eyes, go back to your childhood and think back to all those dreams you had as a child before people started to use the 'no, you can't do that' phrase and began to limit your horizons, your potential, your view of the world. Then answer the question: *'When I grow up, I'm going to be a...'* what? Write down all the things you thought of and then look at what you've written down. Ask yourself:

1. What attracted you to these careers? Which parts are still attractive?
2. How far has your interest in any of those things (in the broadest sense of the word) featured into your adult life?
3. What pulls them together? Creativity? A sense of adventure? Entertaining others? A desire to help the human race?
4. Do they still hang around to tease and sound appealing?
5. Did you ever seriously try to follow them up as a career? If not, what's stopping you now finding out about them?
6. If your dream job is not right for you now, analyse the elements within it which appealed to you originally. For example, if you wanted to become a fireman, what was it about that work which made it your dream job? Was it the sense of adventure, risk taking, being a hero, or danger, or was there anything else which made it your dream job? Which of these elements still appeals to you today? What would your working life be like if your day encompassed them all or some of the time?
7. Pull the commonalities together. Could you see yourself being any of those things at work? If so, what?

Following your heart and hunches

Most decisions made with the heart are successful ones. Decisions made with the head rarely hit the same success rate. Go with your heart. It's important to follow up on hunches, because they often come straight from the heart.

Working with your interests

Why not have a career or job related to your interests? Look for evidence of interest so that you know you're not just kidding yourself, by asking yourself:

1. Given half the chance, what would you talk about endlessly?
2. What are the times you have most enjoyed in your life?
3. What are your hobbies and interests now? Creative? Volunteering? Physical? Social? Practical? Scientific?
4. What were your favourite subjects at school?
5. What do you love reading about?
6. What attracts you to your interests and hobbies?

If you can work in an area where the knowledge you'll need to do the job interests you, it will be much easier and more enjoyable, and your excitement and passion will show as you help clients and customers.

Now think broadly, and ask yourself:

1. What organisations exist to support those interests, issues and concerns? Put down everyone you can think of against each of your interests, even if it does not concentrate exclusively on them. Figure 4 is an example of this sort of exercise.
2. What do they do?
3. What support networks do they have?
4. Could they use your skills, interest and knowledge?
5. Could you set up your own business around them?

The *Yellow Pages* and the Internet, plus voluntary sites such as *www.volunteering.org.uk* will help you connect your interests and passions with organisations. By looking at your interests and listing companies or organisations which are connected with them, you have just identified a large number of employers whom you could approach to see if they could use your skills and abilities. And of course you could always set up your own business!

My interests	Organisations that match those interests
Cats	Pet stores, pet supermarkets RSPCA Cats protection Local cattery Local vet clinic Pet insurers
Listening to people and helping them	Probation service Police force Counselling services Social services Financial advisers Youth service
Working with children	Nurseries, playgroups Schools Ground crew – looking after children at airports Toy shop assistant, store manager Health service specialist Children's clothing store Charity organisation
Food and drink	Teaching cooking to adults at local college Selling at a speciality store Cordon Bleu chef Working in a restaurant Market researcher

Figure 4: Matching potential employers to your interests

Remember that you could run your own business in any of these areas, as well as working for someone else.

Using your talents

If you've got a talent, that's great. If you've got a particular leaning for something, such as painting, music, writing, drawing, dancing and so forth, you may have thought of making a career out of it. The question is, do you use your talent:

- as a leisure pursuit, to enjoy after a day's work;
- as a way to make a living, for example to become a painter, dancer, musician;

- to work in a sector you understand, such as working in the world of music as a band manager; or
- work with it as part of your career, such as being an art teacher, art therapist, or owner of a gallery?

If you decide to turn it into a career, keep focused and working. You never know when the lucky break may come through.

Turning a hobby into a career

Do you relish an interest or hobby sufficiently to make a living out of it, either through starting your own business or working for someone else? Or would you prefer to keep it for pleasure?

Example:	
I love badminton	And I'd love to teach it – I enjoy working with people of all ages. I'd enjoy doing an adult education course and seeing others get pleasure out of something I enjoy doing.
I love badminton	But I couldn't teach it – I'd prefer to keep it as a hobby. It would be too much hassle to teach.
I love boats	And I sell them full time now for a dealer – so I've taken up horse riding at the weekends instead to do something different.
I love boats	But I wouldn't want to get into business with them – they are my hobby!

Case study: Faith, working in a sports complex

'I've always been interested in sports and leisure, and thought it would be fun to work somewhere that people come to because they want to. When I was looking for work, a friend asked me if I'd like to work in a new health centre. I adore it – I love meeting people and working somewhere I'm naturally interested in. I'm going to study for a health promotion qualification next year.'

> It's much easier to keep learning and to provide an excellent service if you're naturally interested in the product and services you're working with.

Who or what do you want to work with?

Consider carefully what – or who – you want to spend most of your time working with:

- *Information and data*
  What sort of information would you like to work with? Think back to your school or college days and your current interest – what appeals to you the most? Economics, statistics, history, science, information technology, geography, mathematics, finance, art, history?

- *Things*
  What sort of things would you like to work with? 'Things' include medicine, plants, buildings, electrics, water, air, the earth, energy, fabrics, colours and food.

- *Ideas*
  Many people work with ideas, whether stories (novelists, for example), anything visual, business ideas, political and religious beliefs and concepts.

- *People*
  The possibilities are so varied that they are considered in greater detail in the next section.

Who do you want to serve?

Most jobs involve contact with people. Do you have a preferred group you'd like to work with? Do any of these particularly make you feel a passionate and instant, *Yes, I'd love to help or work with them!*? Do they make you sit up and feel the 'Wow!' factor?

- The general public
- Teenagers
- Professionals
- Mentally disabled
- Physically disabled
- Teenage mothers
- People with learning difficulties
- The bereaved
- The third age – 50–70
- Sports professionals
- Animals
- Adults seeking work
- Children
- Adults
- The elderly
- Babies
- Parents
- People in prison
- High flyers
- Students
- Tourists
- Other
- Creative people
- Parents-to-be
- Professionals

You can work with these groups of people in many situations:

Do you want to work with people who:	Examples of career areas:
Are ill	Health services, counselling
Are in trouble with the law	Police, probation and prison services, social work, youth and community work
Need love and care	Residential centres, day care centres, homes, hospitals
Want to have fun	Leisure centres, play groups, holidays, hotels, tourists, information centres
Want to get fit	Sports teaching, coaching, personal training instructors
Want advice	Health visiting, counselling, financial institutions, careers counselling
Want to learn	Schools, colleges, universities, WEAs, private colleges and training providers
Need a personal service	Hair, beauty, massage, taxi driving, cleaning, cooking

Wish/need to go on holiday	Travel agencies, package tours, hotels, tourist information centres
Have an emergency	Ambulance driving, police service, fire service, vets
Want to plan for the future	Financial advisers, funeral directors, careers counsellor, insurance, coaches
Wish to buy a product or service	Sales staff, financial adviser, customer service assistants

Within every sector, there will be different levels of staff such as:

- Support staff – PAs, administrators, data entry operators, accounting technicians.
- Front line staff – customer service assistants, receptionists.
- Management – marketing, sales managers, finance directors, accountants, IT specialists.
- Professionals – accountants, vets – anyone who needs professional qualifications in order to practise.
- Associate professionals.

Depending on how much responsibility you want and how much training you are willing to do, one of those levels of work will be more suited to you and your needs than others.

There are lots of other elements to any career; consider them in the next two exercises.

Knowing your values and needs

Exercise

On a separate sheet of paper, copy and complete the questionnaire shown in Figure 5 and put it somewhere you can refer to it easily. It will highlight to you what is important in a job and a company.

Aspects of work that are important to me	Essential	Fairly important	Doesn't matter	Not at all important
To enjoy it and have fun				
The salary – I need to earn £ ___ a month				
Being responsible for other members of staff, a team				
A family-friendly employer				
That I get on well with my colleagues				
Working conditions				
Journey time to work				
Opportunity to meet people				
Customer contact				
Chance to help others				
Hours				
Holiday entitlement				
Good training				
Lots of scope for career progression				
Flexible conditions				
A challenge				
The type of person I would serve				
I can influence the direction of something				
Doesn't involve heights/heat/ dust/dirt/cold				
Feeling valued by colleagues, bosses and customers				
Sense of belonging				

Figure 5: Which aspects of work are important to you?

Using a separate sheet of paper, write down against each trio the aspect mentioned which most appeals to you. This will further your self-knowledge and what's important to you as you return to work:

1. Indoors
    Outdoors
    Mixture

2. Local firm
    National firm
    International firm

3. Large-sized firm
    Medium-sized firm
    Small-sized firm

4. Private sector
    Public organisation
    Charity

5. Lots of deadlines daily
    Very few deadlines at all
    Meeting orders

6. Work for one firm
    Work for several
    Work for self

7. Desk bound
    Car bound
    Moving about

8. Lots of autonomy – can
    handle it on own
    Some autonomy in job
    No autonomy at all – prefer
    to be told what to do

9. To commute to work under
    30 minutes
    Commute to be 30–60 minutes
    Commute irrelevant – it's the
    job that matters

10. Travel around UK for the job
    Travel abroad for the job
    No travelling for the job

11. Performance-related pay
    Salary or wage and commission
    Salary or wage

12. Work from home all the time
    Work out of the house
    Part home-based

13. High profile position in organisation
    Just one of the team
    Work on own

14. Very bureaucratic company
    Some bureaucracy in the company
    No bureaucracy at all

15. Lots of attention to detail
    Some attention to detail
    No detail at all

16. Lots of routine work
    Some routine
    Minimum amount of routine

17. Flexible working day
    Never knowing what is going to
    happen next day
    Knowing exactly what will happen

These exercises will show your gut reaction to what's important to you. Think what's made you make the choices you have and what's behind your motivation to choose them. If any of these elements are particularly important to you, note them.

Knowing what you want helps you to determine your niche at work.

Examples

- Liz knew she didn't want to spend more than 30 minutes getting to work every day – so she concentrated on searching for a job in a large town a bus ride away.
- Eric wanted to work for an international company and didn't mind travelling an hour a day or more to make that happen. As a result, he could consider working in three cities.

Every criterion you place on work reduces your choices. Recognise what matters to you; none of us are as flexible as we like to think we are.

Gather your answers from this chapter together
to start building a picture of what you want to do at work.

Do it now

- Identify what you're passionate about or interested in
- Which sectors are allied to that?
- Who do you want to work with?
- What are your essentials in a job and life?
- Draw a mind-map or brainstorm all the employers you can think of who work in the area.

Summary

You deserve to be happy at work, and do something which is fulfilling and worthwhile.

- Consider who you want to work for and what your true values are.
- Look at organisations which support your values and passions.
- Consider how you can contribute to them.

6

What Do You Want To DO?

If we all did what we are capable of doing, we would literally astound ourselves.

Thomas Edison

This chapter will help you decide what you actually want to *do* at work. There may be particular skills or talents you've got which you want to make the most of. You can apply those to the particular sector you want to work in and make a difference in the most effective way.

Defining work

When people think of the term 'work' they often think in terms of employment, i.e. a job or career.

Work = a job

Or better still:

Work = a paid job.

Work = effort

'Work' covers paid employment, but it also means doing a task or duty which involves a physical or mental effort. Playing tennis requires physical effort and so it's work. So is driving a car, cooking, cleaning, being a member of a committee – they all require physical and mental effort and motivation. The teacher in front of a biology class, the leisurely swimmer in the sea, the Brownie studying for a badge and the man selling raffle tickets to raise money for charity are all working in one way or another, and each is using a different combination of skills and abilities.

You'll need a range of skills at work, including:

- *Basic skills* – literacy, numeracy, plus information technology (i.e. the ability to read, write, do simple sums and use a computer).

- *Transferable skills* – such as communicating, team working, managing yourselves and others. You can find evidence of your abilities in these in running a home, raising a family, travelling, voluntary work, any courses you've done. Anything in fact you've achieved in life will have required the use of transferable skills.

- *Job-specific skills* – these are the skills you need to do a particular job. Filling teeth is a job-specific skill which a dentist needs to be proficient in, for example. Whether you're planning a career change or a return to the workplace, you may need to do some training in job-specific skills to get the career or job you want. Some employers give job-specific training on the job.

- *Management skills* – these relate to self-management – the way you plan your work, prioritise, handle stress and pressure, cope with people and situations – and the management of others, such as you might have had raising children.

- *Leadership skills* – these are all about creating a vision and a strategy to implement that vision. They're about spotting opportunities and building relationships. You'll need these if you want to run your own business or be a leader at work.

Exercise

Make a list of all the activities you do and your achievements to date. These may cover:

- Leisure activities.
- Your achievements, no matter how small you think they are.
- Courses you've done.
- Voluntary work.
- Memberships of organisations or clubs.
- Positions you've held on a committee.
- Kids you've brought up, elderly relatives you've looked after, pets you've cared for.

They'll all have enabled you to develop many skills and abilities. Use your list as you work through the next few chapters to analyse the skills you have and to gather evidence that yes, you *do* have them!

Boosting your basic skills

Can you read and write? Have you got basic mathematical skills? All employers need staff with basic skills so:

> If you find it hard to read, write or do basic maths
> or to use a computer,
> Do Something About It.
> NOW!

If your basic skills are lacking, give Learndirect a call to see what help is in your area. There may be any number of college courses on offer, such as 'Basic Mathematics', or 'Computing for the Terrified' where you can learn in a really friendly and helpful environment. Many jobs are now affected by IT; you don't need to be a computer whiz, you just need to know your way around the keyboard and know how to look after a computer, e.g. not to spill coffee over it. You may already use IT at home, perhaps to order your shopping over the Internet, to do research into a holiday or to send emails to friends and relatives. List everything you use your computer for and you'll be astounded how skilled you are already! The list you draw up is proof of your willingness to embrace IT and show that you can use it. Keep examples of your work – you may be able to use them to gain a National Vocational Qualification (see Chapter 9).

Transferring your skills

Each sector and niche requires skills in common. Many of the skills you use outside work can be transferred across the workplace. Let's take some examples.

Excelling at communicating

Checklist everyone you've communicated with this week:

- Who were they?
- How did you communicate?
- What sort of language and tone did you adopt?
- How many were on a business basis (e.g. the gas or phone company)?
- How do you think the other person felt after the communication between you?
- What did you achieve as a result of the communication between you?

Think of the times when you've presented a case to somebody, done some public speaking, complained about a service or product, given constructive criticism, negotiated (for example with your children), dealt with a conflict, handled a sensitive situation, participated in a meeting and so on. Communication also involves delegating tasks to others sometimes – such as your children to clear the table or wash the dishes. It also involves listening. In many jobs you need the ability to listen to what people are not telling you as much as what they are saying. Giving people time to explain their needs – and complaints if they have them – is vital.

Looking after our customers

Customer care is crucial – we need to know how to look after those who use our services and products because they could go elsewhere if they're not happy with the way we treat them. A warm welcome, a smile, plenty of eye contact and a positive approach make a difference to a customer's impression of a company. We need to go the extra mile wherever we can to encourage our customers to recommend us to others and to ensure they keep coming back for more.

Delivering what you promise

Being nice to customers means nothing if you don't do what you said you would do for them. Think of a time when one company met a deadline over something that was important to you and another when a company didn't.

1. How did you feel about the company that did deliver?
2. How did you feel about the one that didn't make it?
3. Which would you use again in the future?

Do you always deliver what you say you will? How often? 100% of the time? 80%? 50%? Not at all? What do you think *your* customers will expect from you?

Showing you can handle routine

Every job has routine tasks, whatever level you're working at. Currently, your routine tasks may include:

- Shopping
- Washing and ironing
- Cooking
- Caring for pets, children, the elderly
- Dealing with bills and budgeting

Even routine tasks demand manual dexterity – strong and supple hands. You use organisational skills to manage your time, working out what needs to be done first and dealing with interruptions as they occur. You constantly motivate yourself – things won't get done if you slump in front of the television – and you persuade and motivate others, such as your children to tidy their rooms. You work without supervision and just get on with things – as you would at work.

Making good use of time

How good are you at organising yourself and prioritising your time? Can you easily spot your priorities during the day, the week, the month and the year? Do you plan well ahead or leave everything until the last minute? Can you take on a project and work on it in the right and logical order so that it gets finished on time, delegating along the way where appropriate?

Working in a team

Some people are natural team players. They participate in team sports, play their role on committees, look forward to working with other people and doing their bit. They have their own principles and views, but are prepared to compromise when necessary in favour of the bigger picture. If they are suddenly asked to join a team to get something done – for example to take part in organising a jumble sale to raise money quickly to send to earthquake victims on the other side of the world – they are happy to jump in at once and do what they can, working well alongside people they don't necessarily know.

Other people are distinctly uncomfortable doing things in a group and prefer to do things on their own. Visiting the cinema or theatre, swimming, cycling or cooking are all activities that can be done alone – they don't need anyone else to be involved.

Many of us combine solo and team activities. Margaret loves a game of tennis with her three friends but she also loves knitting. She has a wide span of interests which shows an employer that she's a team player but also someone who can do things on her own.

- How many of your activities involve working with a group of people, either for leisure or interest or as a volunteer?
- How much do you enjoy working with others in a team to achieve a goal? Can you show that you have done this in the past? What was your contribution?
- Describe something you have done in a team recently. What part did you play? What problems were there in the team and how did you work to overcome them?

If you do not enjoy working with others, look for a job which doesn't involve much contact with them. But ask yourself why you don't enjoy it: are you very shy, for example, or do you lack confidence? Would an assertiveness course or coaching help you overcome those issues?

Are you a leader?

Team activities can give you good insight into the role you want – whether you like to be the leader of the pack or prefer to play a supporting part. When you are working in a team of people what sort of role do you prefer to play? Do you automatically find yourself seeking to take charge and lead a project, pulling people together and ensuring that everything is running smoothly. If you like to run the show, why not think about running your own business?

Managing yourself

Self-management skills are crucial to a happy life, in and out of work. They cover areas such as:

- career/working life
- health and stress
- time – making sure you meet deadlines, for example
- workload – working out what needs to be done when
- prioritising – what should come first?

- negotiating – with a range of people
- conflict
- training needs
- decision making
- budgeting.

> Throughout your life, you'll have developed a broad range of skills and abilities which can be applied to the workplace.

Case study: June, looking after the family

If you've been looking after the family for years, you feel you're invisible – the behind-the- scenes person who holds everything together without anyone realising you're there. You clean, iron, wash, cook, shop, sort out bills, insurance, look after people when they're ill – but do you feel valued and appreciated?

The examples below show further how skills transfer from life to work.

Skill used at work	Examples of how you use it in life
Communicating in writing	Writing letters, completing forms
Communicating orally	Calling round to organise a party
Team working	Voluntary work
Organising	Dinner party, jumble sale
Planning	Specific event in the future e.g. holiday
Juggling	Doing several things at once in a hurry
Prioritising	Deciding what needs to be done first
Budgeting	For something specific e.g. a new car, or routine, e.g. the shopping
Researching information	Schools for the kids, where you want to live

Negotiating	With the kids about times they come home
Persuading	People to do things they might not want to do
Leading	A group, the family, a football team
Creating	Ideas of things for the kids to do on a rainy day
Recruiting	Plumber, electrician, baby sitter, cleaner
Selling things	Raffle tickets, flag day
Motivating others	The kids to tidy their room or wash the car
Stamina	Keeping going from dawn to midnight!

Example: Planning a holiday

You use many skills at Christmas or any other festive time, such as:

- *Negotiating with the family* – where will you go and when?
- *Planning* – what to take, activities to do, the journey to the airport or port, what needs to be done before you go.
- *Workload* – how you're going to fit in everything you need to do before you leave.
- *Conflict* – handling the usual family arguments, if you have any.
- *Training needs* – would it be useful to learn the language of the country you're visiting?
- *Time* – making the most of the time you've got while you're away.
- *Prioritising* – what needs to be done first: book the holiday or the cattery?
- *Health and stress* – how can you make the journey less stressful, especially if you've got young kids?

- *Decision-making* – understanding how you make decisions and how your process may be different from your partner's!

- *Budgeting* – how much can you afford to spend on this holiday?

- *Researching information* – what will there be to do in the day? What will the hotel be like?

- *Persuading* – kids are very good at this. *Hey, Dad, please can we have another day at Disneyland tomorrow? P l e a s e!* Watch your kids' technique and learn.

- *Creating* – ways to lessen the boredom of a long journey e.g. creating car games for the kids.

You can put all your transferable skills to the test by undertaking work experience and voluntary work.

Exercise

You need skills to manage your whole life. If you don't believe me, look back at your day yesterday. How many of the above skills did you use as far as yesterday was concerned?

Using job-specific skills

Every job has specific skills it alone needs, in addition to the transferable ones everybody uses. The job-specific skills demanded by a public relations person and a butcher are different.

Which job-specific skills do you want to use at work?

Acting	Analysing	Building
Administering	Answering questions	Caring for others
Assembling	Arguing	Checking facts/
Assessing	Assimilating	figures
Advising	Book-keeping	Classifying
Advocating	Budgeting	Coaching

Comparing	Identifying	Questioning
Conducting	opportunities	Reading
Controlling	Implementing	Recalling
Co-ordinating	Initiating	Recording
Copying	Inspecting	Recruiting
Counselling	Intervening	Registering
Creating	Interviewing	Regulating
Cultivating	Investigating	Relaying information
Debating	Investing	Renewing
Demolishing	Keeping records	Repairing
Demonstrating	Leading	Reporting
Designing	Learning	Researching
Developing	Listening	Reviewing
People	Lobbying	Seeking advice
Ideas	Managing	Selling
Products	Marketing	Serving others
Dispensing	Massaging	Showing
Displaying	Mediating	Solving problems
Drafting	Mending	Supervising
Drawing	Monitoring	Supporting
Driving	Motivating others	Talking
Editing	Navigating	Taking minutes
Empathising	Negotiating	Teaching
Establishing	Networking	Telephoning
something	Organising	Thinking rapidly
Examining	Persuading others	Touching
Explaining	Presenting	Tracing
Financing	Prioritising	Training
Fund-raising	Probing	Transferring
Generating business	Processing	Transporting
Giving	Promoting	Travelling
Greeting	Proving	Tutoring
Growing	Protecting	Understanding
Guiding	Public speaking	Underwriting
Handling	Publishing	Welcoming
	Purchasing	Writing

Which of these skills would the following people particularly need to do their jobs:

- teacher
- film editor
- journalist
- designer?

Some jobs use one skill more than others; a nurse might teach a patient how to give himself an injection, whereas a teacher teaches a class much of the time.

Most jobs involve several skills with an emphasis on one or two very specific ones. A counsellor spends most of her time counselling people – but she needs to keep her records up to date, market her own service to professionals and liaise with other people in the medical profession about her patients. The emphasis for her, however, will be on the counselling.

Exercise

1. From the list of skills above, note down which ones you:

- Use regularly.
- Are good at using.
- Enjoy using.
- Want to use on the job.
- Haven't had a chance to use before but would love to try.
- Would love to do in work.

2. Now limit those further to three top skills you want to do all day. How can you refresh those skills if you already have them, or train to do them if you don't?

This will help you to determine what you actually want to *do* all day.

Being an entrepreneur

Many people start their own business for the flexibility they think it will bring, or the desire to work for themselves. Others are hungry to get a great idea they've got off the ground. You need to have a clear idea of where your company is going and what you want to achieve, and who you're going to serve, and with what products and services you'll serve them. You need to know which part of the market you're gunning for and how you differ from your competitors. You also need to take a big picture view, yet be able to pay attention to detail.

Advantages of working for yourself include:

- It may be easier to balance work and family life.
  I need to pick the kids up after school, so I'll block that out of my diary.

- More choice in your working hours.
  It's 3am and I'm still working to ensure everything is ready for tomorrow's meeting.

- It's very satisfying to have your own business (when things are going well).
  At least I get to say what's what.

- You can work from home.
  A thirty-second commute...no more standing on cold wet platforms waiting for the 7.48 train.

Disadvantages include:

- The hours can be very long and the holidays few or non-existent.
  You go skiing, darling. I can't take the time off.

- It can be very lonely.
  Well, Tiddles and Fido, what do you think our sales strategy should be next year?

- The business could fail.
  Then what?

● It may be difficult to 'leave the office' especially if you work from home.

I'll just see if there are any emails before I go to bed.

If you're planning on setting up your own business, talk to those you live with first. Your life as a budding entrepreneur will certainly impact on them.

So are you an entrepreneur?

Are you:

Entrepreneurial	____	Energetic	____
Determined	____	Prepared to delegate	____
Focused	____	Able to work on your own	____
A risk taker	____	Willing to forgo holidays at first	____
A clear thinker	____	Full of stamina	____
Resilient	____	Competitive	____
Tough	____	Highly organised	____
Creative	____	Able to spot gaps in the market	____
Willing to work hard	____	Full of self-belief and confidence	____
A networker	____	Highly motivated	____

If you're checking most boxes yes, then consider going self-employed. If not, stick to working for someone else. Of course, you can be employed in one job and self-employed in another.

Managing and making things happen

Entrepreneurs have the vision and then go about making it happen. Managers implement that vision and set it up and run it. Leaders have overall responsibility for the performance of the company or organisation, and if it falls foul of the law, they will be held accountable. Managers implement strategies and regulations. They take control and carry out The Plan. They may specialise in a number of different fields, such as:

Human resources	Information technology
Projects	Marketing
Sales	Disaster
Product development	Property
Facilities	Event and conference

They may also however be generalist, covering a wide range of aspects.

The numbers of managers vary, depending on the size of the organisation. Strong people skills are essential: you need to be able to motivate others to achieve an end goal and to perform at high standards. You also need to understand how new legislation in the workplace may affect your team and what policies your company has for areas such as personal Internet use at work, for example. A good human resource and IT department will guide and support you. Make friends with them early on!

There is a whole host of qualifications in management, many of which are in the areas mentioned above, and there are a number of organisations out there which are dedicated to helping managers or would-be managers network or boost their competence and confidence in the role they have.

Providing the hands-on

If you provide the know-how, you've got the knowledge and skills necessary to perform a particular role in an organisation at a specific level. You're unlikely to have the big picture view, and may simply regard your role as a job, going in from 9 to 5 and not thinking very much about it after you go home. That doesn't mean you don't take pride in your work! Strong customer service skills and attention to detail are probably key factors. Examples include:

Book-keeper	Craftsman
Carpenter	Hairdresser
Data entry operator	Waitress
Designer	Beauty therapist

Of course, all these aforementioned roles can be done by you as the owner of your own business, in which case you'd also need entrepreneurial flair and management abilities.

You may need to combine these roles!

Many people at this level run their own business. A hairdresser decides to go it alone. She needs a vision of where her business is going; the management abilities to make that happen; and the know-how to do the work. She needs to take a step back to look at the bigger picture and may need to delegate some of the hands-on work to concentrate on business development. Managerial skills are important – to keep to budget and time while adhering to health and safety regulations. She could in time own a number of salons and employ staff to do the hands-on type work.

Considering results

What results do you want to see at the end of your endeavours? Who do you want them to affect?

- Individuals
- Organisations
- Communities
- Charities.

This can make a huge difference. If you want to help an individual for example, you could counsel someone who has suffered a bereavement or wants to change career; equally you could find yourself making a decision on a strategy which affects a number of people in combination. When you're job hunting, you'll need to show prospective employers that you can achieve results.

How do you want your work to be measured?

Consider the outcome you want your efforts at work to have. Examples are:

- Targets
- Influencing policy
- Developing people
- Financial rewards

- Recognition for a job well done
- Securing a contract
- Coming up with a new product
- New structure, such as a furniture piece
- A new look
- Creating policies
- Profits

- Deals
- Promotion
- Seeing your idea come into being
- Having a positive influence on someone
- Influencing the direction of something
- Happy customers
- A sale

- Setting up a new system

- Administering justice
- Developing a successful team

Deciding what you want

Before you make your key decision about what you're going to do, ask yourself these questions to help you check you're on the right track:

- What is most important to me in this move back to work?
- What am I prepared to compromise over? How much?
- If I were to look forward to my retirement day, what would I want to look back on?
- What do I see myself doing in 5 years' time? What sort of organisation and employer would enable me to achieve that?
- Who do I want to work for?
- What is my heart telling me to do?
- If I could start a career totally afresh, what would it be?
- Where is my home in the workplace? Which sector do I want to work in?
- What do I want to contribute?

Start to mould your answers into a picture of what you want to do, and you can start finding out more about it, to see if you like what you're hearing and are excited by it.

The best route to get what you want may be to start your own business.

Do it now

- What did you do in your break from the workplace? Identify three things you did and then pinpoint transferable skills you used to make them happen.
- What job specific skills do you want to use?
- How far do you see leadership, entrepreneurial and management skills featuring in your next role?
- What results do you want to achieve?

Summary

Within the workplace, every sector has specialists who have a niche.

- They use specific job-related skills which they have usually been trained for.

- They have a particular position in the organisation – to provide a vision, or manage the implementation of that vision; or do the work required to make the business function.

- They cater for a particular group of customers – their preferred group.

7

Tried and Tested...You Plc, Them Plc

‘Research will help you determine whether your next move is right for you.’

It's time to work out where you fit into the workplace. Maybe you already know; but this chapter will help you to start making contacts and ensure that you're heading in the right direction. Of key importance will be the amount of training you are prepared to put in, and what the job opportunities are in your area, because you may need to be more flexible than you had originally hoped. Make the most of the help available to you, and network, network, network. This means getting out of the house and meeting people.

The more you check things out and get a 'feel' for 'yes, that's me!', the better position you'll be in to make a solid positive career choice that's right for you. If you start getting excited by what you see and feel around you, you know you're heading for the right place.

Knowing yourself

Key to success in any career move is how well you know yourself, what you want and what you've got to offer. Consider your:

- aspirations
- goals
- likes
- values
- strengths
- desire for responsibility
- desire to achieve
- likes
- strengths – what are you good at?
- what's important to you in your career.

You'll notice that all these things focus on what you do want, as opposed to what you don't.

What else?

You also need to consider any restrictions which are going to be placed on you. For example:

- where you live will affect the employment opportunities to work for someone else, unless you do it from home

- your health – certain allergies may prohibit you from following certain careers, for example

- your willingness to travel to work. Commuting long distances every day or week will bring more opportunities within your reach

- your view of your 'ideal employer'.

Now that you've done all this research into what *you* want, it's time to decide what sector you want to work in and what skills you want to use in it. Before you start, sum up what you want.

Describing yourself

1. Using the information you have acquired so far about yourself, write a personal summary about what you're looking for in your next role along the lines outlined in Stage 1 in Figure 3 on pp. 28 and 29.

   Concentrate on:

   - what you want to do and achieve;
   - your career and life aspirations;
   - why you want to go back to work;
   - the skills you have and the qualities you can offer;
   - the sector you most want to work in;
   - the key elements to you;
   - the sort of work you are looking for and the kind of organisation you want to work for.

2. Now find the answers to Stages 2–5 in Figure 3 in Chapter 3 on pp. 28 and 29 by continuing on with Chapter 9 to 15 to complete the rest of the activities you need to do to make your career move happen by working your way through the next few chapters.

Key questions to ask

Talk with as many people 'in the field' as you can to update yourself or prove that a change of career is right for you. If you're setting up your own business, you need to understand the world you'll be running a business in, and what makes your customers and suppliers and so forth tick.

Make good use of your network

Ask everyone you know whether they have any contacts who could:

- help you find more information

- offer you work experience
- advise you on your CV – is it appropriate for the sector?
- tell you more about the industry
- give you ideas about how you can get to where you want to be.

Questions to ask include...

Remember that not all the questions will be relevant to you, but here are some you may want to find the answers to.

What is a typical day at work like?
Could I happily do that every day?

How did you train for this work?
Am I prepared to spend that amount of time training?

Can I do this sort of work from home?
Could I organise myself and my family enough to make this work?

Can I do this on a part-time basis?
Will it provide me with sufficient income for my needs?

What skills and qualities does this work demand?
Do I have them? What would I need to do to train up in them?

What are the advantages and disadvantages of entering this career through this route?
How do I feel about those?

Who are the main employers in my area?
Are they expanding or down-sizing?
How do their values match mine?

What do people enjoy most about working in this sector?
Does that appeal to me?

How did you establish your own business?
Could I do that?

Who helped you set up your own business? Who provided the best advice and support?
Get in touch with them to talk them through my ideas.

Is this sector very competitive to get into? Will a stint of unpaid work experience boost my chances of success? What will give me an edge?
Am I prepared to do what it takes to get in?

Who do I know who works in the sector? Who do I know who might know someone working in the sector?
When am I going to get in touch with them to ask if I can have a discussion with them about my plans?

Is there any chance I could get some work experience or do some work shadowing for a day or so, or more?
I must identify exactly what I want to get out of it.

What's the best way 'in' for someone like me who is new to the field, or who wants to get back in it?
Am I prepared to do what it takes?

How does this sector recruit staff?
How should I adapt my CV to suit it?
What will I need to do to get a foot in the door?

Can my contacts suggest anyone else I could talk to?
I must make time to give them a call.

How are people employed? How much scope is there for setting up on my own?
Does this appeal to me and my needs?

What are this sector's strengths and weaknesses?
Do they excite or worry me?

What are the challenges it faces at the moment?
How would I rise to those challenges and do they concern me?

Questions relating to current training and qualifying may best be left to the professional bodies who will be up to date on what's required for membership or to work in the sector.

Ask for an informal meeting

You could ask people you have met recently to arange for an informal meeting to get answers to these questions. If you write to ask for such a meeting, don't send your CV – it will look as if you want a job. For the purpose of this meeting, you simply want information and advice. If a friend gave the person you're contacting their name, mention them. Keep the letter short, but give them a brief idea of what you're after and the research you've done so far. Most people are pleased to help – it gives them a boost and shows them to be people who know what they are talking about. Meetings like this will put you ahead of the pack when it comes to applying for positions – it shows you are serious about your career and future. Don't forget to write and thank anyone who helps you for their time and advice.

Assembling your essential toolkit: resources

There are many practical resources available to help you. Don't forget your local Jobcentre Plus, careers services, colleges and training providers who can point you in the right direction.

Network, network, network

You come into contact with all sorts of people from different sectors every day, be they family, friends, relatives, friends of friends and professionals such as doctors and dentists.

Exercise

Start assembling your networks of people. Figure 6 shows you all the people you could include on your list.

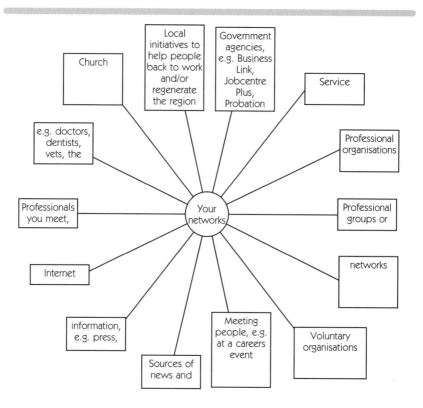

Figure 6. Boost your network

When you take into account that all the people you can name in any of these areas will have their own networks, you can start to see the power of talking to people about your future plans. Do they know of someone who could really open doors for you?

Many vacancies are filled by employers taking on people who've been recommended to them by current or past employees whom they highly value. In fact, many employers pay their staff bounties for successful new recruits they bring to the company. So your network of people can help you by:

1. Leading you to employers who may be recruiting or show an interest in your CV.
2. Leading you to people who can advise, inform, counsel, coach, facilitate and encourage you in your return to work. These include:
   - people at work who can tell you what it's like from day to day to be in the job they're in
   - training providers such as colleges, private companies, universities
   - recruitment agencies, Jobcentre Plus offices
   - professional bodies who can advise on qualifications, training and career opportunities for their specific area of work
   - help groups, especially for people setting up their own business, such as lunch clubs, networking groups.

You've probably already used your network to get information you need to help you make an informed decision, such as finding the right school for your kids and looking for a reputable plumber. For the purpose of returning to work, your network isn't so much about asking people for a job, as for information about careers, employment, training and education opportunities.

Networking has its own protocol, including:

Dos	Don'ts
Think up questions to ask people prior to meeting them.	Ask for or demand a job, or be pushy if you don't get the help you want.
Thank people for any help they give you.	Assume that everything you're told is up to date, especially if you're getting the information from friends or family. Professional bodies will have the up-to-date information you need.
Remember the way you behave towards those they recommend you talk to reflects on them.	Be swayed or manipulated by others.

Offer to return the favour some day.

> Be prepared to create your own network or add to your existing one by picking up the phone, emailing people and digging about to reach the people you need to contact.

An understanding of IT can help

The Internet is an important job-hunting tool, with a great deal of information about education, employment, training and self-employment opportunities on it. You can access the Internet at your local college, careers service, library and Jobcentre Plus office to research:

- *Actual jobs* – many agencies have web sites and there are a lot of agencies which operate on line.

- *Information about specific companies* – most companies have their own web site with careers or 'work for us' pages.

- *Education institutions* – most colleges and universities are now on the Net and you can use sites such as *www.learndirect.co.uk*, *www.ucas.com* and *www.hotcourses.com* to find your nearest course.

- *Information on practical support* if you need it, such as child care, employers of the disabled, mature workers.

- *Information on running your own business*, with details of support in your area.

- *Advice for specific groups on returning to work*, such as women returners, offenders, those who've had heart problems or cancer.

- *Details of career networking groups for returners* and any return to work courses run by professional organisations.

- *Details of professional organisations and bodies* and of the training offered in their industries, together with details of careers and jobs.

Learn how to use the Internet

It's invaluable; your local college will have details of courses available or you can check on *www.learndirect.co.uk* for details.

Practical resources

You'll need some practical things to help you plot your return to work. You can access some of these at your local Jobcentre Plus office, careers service or public library without having to buy them.

- A word processor for compiling and sending CVs, letters of application, emailing.
- An outfit suitable for meetings, careers events, networking lunches, recruitment fairs, interviews; a suit and shirt or blouse, with tidy, well heeled and polished shoes will suffice.
- Financial resources, such as a bank account (for your salary!), for travel to and from work, coffee and tea in some organisations, tax and national insurance, care costs for dependants you have.
- Your NI number and P45 to give to your new employer. If you've never worked, go to your local tax office for help.

Time, energy and persistence

Put time aside each day to work on your career plan and make this return to work happen. Give yourself time to visualise what life will be like when you start back. How will you feel? What difference will it make to your finances? What will you spend the money on? Who might you meet along the way?

Case Study: Maggie, now a proofreader working from home

'I thought about my day and the time when I'm at my most positive. I'm a morning person, so I put an hour aside every morning after my husband left

> the house to do my career planning. It worked well for me, because I did it before starting all the mundane tasks which left me feeling I was just a housewife.'

Finally, you need the commitment and persistence to keep going, even when you get knocked back a couple of steps. Job hunting is like a game of chess: you need to have a strategy to achieve what you want, but you may lose some pieces along the way.

 # Finding reliable resources

A great place to start to find reliable information is with the professional organisations and the Business Link network if you want to start your own business. Learning and Skills Councils are responsible for the planning and funding of education and training for all adults in England.

Recruitment agencies

These have huge insight into job opportunities within a given sector and they should be able to advise you on:

- Writing a CV.
- Handling interviews.
- Salary checks.
- Profiles of satisfied clients – both employers and candidates.
- Their history and track record in a given industry.
- Names of their consultants.
- Current vacancies they are trying to fill.
- Advice on the best way 'in'.
- What you need to do to boost your chances of success.
- Your personal presentation.

Check out company web sites

Many companies have a web site from which you can gather a great deal such as:

- An introduction to the company, usually on the 'About Us' page.

- A history of the company.

- The management structure.

- The products and services it offers – do they excite you?

- An outline of their vision for the future – does it make you think 'I *really* want to be a part of that'?

- News and press releases.

- Lots of financial information.

- Details on the location(s) of the company with a map of how to get there – helpful if you're going to an interview.

- A guide to its ethos and values – do they hit a chord with you?

- Initiatives which help employees at work, such as moves to help staff achieve the work–life balance they want.

- Documents such as the Annual Report.

- A links page to other relevant sites.

- Any community issues the company is involved with.

- Profiles of individuals working for the organisation.

Within each company, there will be someone with responsibility for human resources, i.e. the people. In large organisations, this could involve an entire department of staff, each with their own area to look after. In smaller companies, this may mean the Office Manager/ PA and Boss.

Contacting employers

You can make contact with employers by phone, snail mail (that's the post), email or via their web site on which you'll find:

- a contact-us section;

- a page for recruitment (which could be named Jobs, Work for us! Recruitment, Careers) with information on how to apply;

- possibly a chat page where you can chat to employees;

- possibly a test to see if you'd have the right sort of qualities and character to fit in.

Attending careers fairs

Careers fairs are a great way to meet employers. They attend careers fairs to meet potential candidates.

To prepare for a careers fair, have you:

- Found out who'll be attending before you go, and researched them? ☐

- Checked to see if they have been in the news recently? ☐

- What messages are you picking up about the organisation's values and ethics, community spirit and career opportunities? ☐

- Prepared up-to-date copies of your CV to take with you? ☐

- Got ready to talk about your next move in a positive way and comment on what you can offer? ☐

- Dressed as if you were going for an interview?

And a checklist for while you're there:

- Go to the stands which interest you the most when you're freshest. You can always wander around at leisure afterwards. ☐

- Don't hog the people you're talking to. Make contact, talk to them about what you're looking for and what you have to offer, and ask them about any opportunities they have. Mention any research you've done into their organisation. ☐

- Sign up for any talks and sessions on offer giving advice about writing a CV, interview technique, or what it's like to work in a particular sector. ☐

After the event:

- Reflect on what you've learnt and how that all fits into your career plans. ☐

- Record the names you've acquired from business cards and conversations into your address book. ☐

- Email or write to anyone you particularly want to follow up to thank them for their time and help. If you want to take them further, ask them what the next step is. Could you meet them for a longer discussion? ☐

- Work out what to do next. If you don't do anything, you'll stay where you are. ☐

Careers fairs are usually advertised in the local press, or your Jobcentre Plus should have details on forthcoming events.

Tapping into professional organisations

Most careers have professional associations or bodies which set the standards and behaviour expected of their members and which also lay down the structure and content of the training required to join their ranks. Log onto the web site for a professional body and you can expect to find information on:

- An overview of the industry, including future needs.

- Careers specific to it.

- Profiles of individuals in different roles, so that you can see what the roles would involve.

- Qualifications and training courses plus possibly details of funding and links to colleges and training providers offering the courses.

- Any continuing professional development requirements.
- Placement opportunities.
- Recruitment services.
- Advice for people who want to change career and move into the industry.
- Details of any refresher groups or training for people who want to return to work.
- Opportunities for self-employment within the sector.
- Details of national, regional and local networks.
- Events coming up.
- Discussion forums – why not email and ask for advice as a returner?
- Advice for people with particular needs.
- News from the sector.
- Campaigns being run.
- Frequently asked questions.
- Possibly, vacancies employers in the sector are seeking to fill.
- Links to other useful bodies.
- Further contact details.

Many professional bodies have their own e-magazine, newspaper or publication – a *must read* if you're to find out what's happening. Before you order them from your newsagent, find out whether the magazines are available on-line, or whether you can read them in your public library's reference section.

Such reading material enables you to learn about trends in the sector, what the current issues and challenges are, and which skills shortages there are. They give you something to refer to when you're talking to employers, and show that you're seriously interested. They give you great tips in terms of how the sector recruits and may point to gaps in the market you could fill with your own business.

Do it now

- Write up your career goal, describing what sort of role you want by when.
- Find out as much as you can about the industry through research.
- Research what you will need to do to be successful.
- Use your network to start making contacts who can help you.
- What sort of employer are you looking for?

Summary

There are so many different niche areas in the workplace, you should either be able to match your career aspirations to one of them or spot a gap you can fill in terms of the services or products you can provide as your own business.

- Make sure the information you are getting is up to date by contacting relevant professional bodies as well as people working in the field.

- Be aware of opportunities locally and further afield to find out about different sectors and careers.

- Identify the skills, attitude and approach those sectors want. Can you meet them?

8

It's Your Business

You've got control. Entirely.

Taking affairs into your own hands and running your own business is an excellent way to take firm control of your working life. You don't have to stick to a clientele that's locally based, either. Depending on what your services are, your clients could be over the other side of the world. The person living on a small island with a computer and Internet access can run a business from home just as well as the individual living in Cardiff, Sheffield or Paris.

Where do you start?

You may already have a great idea for your business in mind. Here are some questions to consider:

1. Why do you want to run your own business?
2. What do you want your business to do?
3. What do you want it to achieve? What is its potential and what are its future prospects?
4. What will you bring to the business and what will you do about any gaps in your business expertise and knowledge?

5. What will your niche be?
6. Who will your competitors be and how will you differ from them? What are your unique selling points?
7. How much money will you need to get your business off the ground and where will that capital come from? How will you live while it gets going?
8. How are you going to market your business?
9. Who will your customers be? How will you make sure you keep them?
10. What image do you want your business to portray? What values will it reflect?
11. Where will you run the business?
12. How does having your own business fit in with family life?

There will be others, and it would be worth looking to see what workshops and short courses are on offer in your area to help you make sure you cover all the points. Many of these courses are run by government agencies, and some are targeted at specific groups, such as women in rural areas. Your local government's web site, plus that of your local Business Link (more on that in a minute) will have details.

Figure 7 shows how to proceed once you've got your idea.

Knowing why businesses fail

According to the Business Link web site, 20% of new businesses fold within the first year, so forewarned is forearmed. Common mistakes people make include:

1. Poor or inadequate market research; people just don't do enough research into their business idea and its viability; they don't get objective feedback or find out enough about clients and the marketplace.
2. Weak financial planning: they lack capital, a contingency plan and are reluctant to seek professional advice.
3. Making unrealistic forecasts about their business's potential.

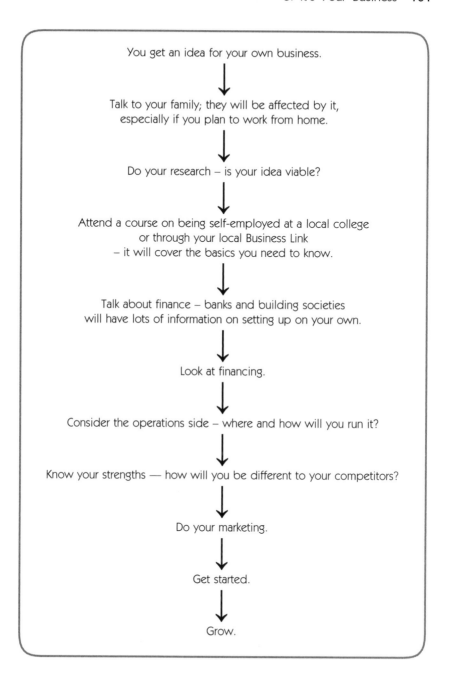

You get an idea for your own business.

↓

Talk to your family; they will be affected by it,
especially if you plan to work from home.

↓

Do your research – is your idea viable?

↓

Attend a course on being self-employed at a local college
or through your local Business Link
– it will cover the basics you need to know.

↓

Talk about finance – banks and building societies
will have lots of information on setting up on your own.

↓

Look at financing.

↓

Consider the operations side – where and how will you run it?

↓

Know your strengths — how will you be different to your competitors?

↓

Do your marketing.

↓

Get started.

↓

Grow.

Figure 7. Planning your own business

4. Forgetting to watch the competition – you need to be able to respond to competitors and new developments.
5. Failing to choose suppliers carefully and setting up satisfactory credit arrangements.
6. Tying up capital through poor stock control and an over-investment in fixed assets.
7. Hiring the wrong people or hiring people in the wrong way and failing to delegate because you want to control everything yourself. You need to be able to stand back and take a view of where the business is and where it is going.

> There's lots of advice, information and help on offer so make the most of it. Don't bury your head in the sand.

What's the make up of businesses in your area?

If a lot of companies or businesses in your area are small (i.e. under 50 people) and you have particular skills they might be able to use by taking you on freelance, why not set up on your own? It's a great way to put all your skills and experience to use. Just think of all the skills small businesses could use by enlisting services freelance, as opposed to the hassle of taking someone on:

- human resources
- secretarial services
- IT
- web design
- marketing
- PR
- training and development
- coaching and mentoring
- event planning
- product design
- business development and growth
- image consulting
- sales.

You can learn a lot about your region's economic make-up by visiting the Regional Development Agency's web site for your region. Twelve RDAs exist throughout the UK, all dedicated to boosting their region's competitiveness and sustainable economic growth, along with quality of life.

Accessing support to start up

There are many groups you can turn to for help, advice and support when you're setting up your own business. Those who seek help and advice from the start are more likely to be successful.

Banks and building societies

You can get lots of helpful information from banks and building societies – some are more dedicated to small businesses than others. They may have booklets and advisers to get you going – simply walk into your nearest branch and ask. Don't waste loyalty on sticking to your own bank or building society – visit a few until you find one you feel comfortable with and which can meet your needs.

Business Link

The Business Link site (*www.businesslink.gov.uk*) has lots of information and advice, with helpful, practical and easily read articles. According to the Small Business Service, in 2003, Business Link helped over 430,000 businesses *and* 170,000 individuals thinking of starting a business. Each local Business Link has its own name and web site. These contain a huge amount of business information and advice, with helpful, practical and easily read articles on areas such as:

- Starting a business, e.g. buying a franchise, getting grants, writing a business plan or forming a business.
- Growing a business.
- Managing a business.

- Exiting a business.
- International trade.
- Sales and marketing.
- IT and e-commerce.
- Compliance.
- People and employment.
- Funding.

Business Link organisations provide the perfect one-stop-shop if you're setting up your own business, with advisers, on-line help and free-phone numbers. The services on offer vary around the country, but may include help with health and safety, communications, energy, human resources, legal matters, tax issues, accounting and marketing. Some services may be available to members only.

Most Business Link organisations have regular newsletters to keep you well up to date with what's going on in your area, such as networks, for example some are sector specific, with speakers talking on subjects absolutely relevant to the sector, seminars and work-shops, which are theme related, training events on a range of subjects, such as 'How to turn an angry customer into a loyal one,' road shows and exhibitions.

HM Revenue and Customs

This department has a huge web site with a great deal of information on it for individuals and employers alike. It runs very useful workshops throughout the UK covering subjects such as 'Becoming Self-Employed' and 'Self-Assessment for the Self-Employed' and taking the fear and mystery out of the being self-employed so far as tax and VAT goes. To register is simple: you simply call a helpline and give them your National Insurance number. It's surprisingly quick and easy, and you can also do it on-line. Business support teams are available to help you understand what you need to do when you're starting a business. Get in touch and see what they've got to offer.

Find out what your local government is doing

Many local government agencies run drop-in days, workshops and events, to give you access under one roof to a whole host of experts who can answer any questions you have. There may be stands of accountants, banks and building societies, HM Revenue and Customs, training providers, web designers, marketing professionals, agencies such as Business Link and so on, all of whom are ready to help you set up your own business. Side sessions may be on offer with sessions on 'Setting up your own business' and you will probably have the opportunity to hear from people – like you – who've done it.

You should also find out what facilities are on offer locally for people running their own business. These could come in the guise of business incubation units in business parks and access to shared office space and secretarial support.

Check out New Deal

If you're currently unemployed, look into New Deal. There's a special programme for people who want to set up their own business. Your local Jobcentre Plus office will have more details, and there's a phone number and web site at the back of this book under Useful Addresses.

Learn from people who've succeeded

Take any opportunity you can to benefit from the advice and lessons others have learnt in setting up their own businesses. There are many events designed to help budding entrepreneurs, so make the most of them. Most have lots of stands manned by people who have products and services and advice to offer you, but there are usually talks and sessions on a variety of subjects, such as confidence building, how to market your business and so on.

Join networking groups

These are plentiful and they range from the specialist groups to the more generalist. Examples are:

- Women In Rural Enterprises (for women who run their own businesses in rural areas)

- everywoman.co.uk

- Business Networking International which has chapters throughout the UK

- ecademy.com

You can find networks local to you by searching the Internet – put your county and business networks into Google, for example – and checking your local Business Link and council sites.

Groups such as these can help in areas such as confidence, personal development, business skills courses and expertise, networking groups, news and information. They are a great way to stop feeling isolated if you're working on your own.

Considering how to work

You've got a number of choices when setting up, including:

Purchasing a franchise

This enables you to acquire the backing and experience of the franchisor who wants to set up in your area. You should get training and the opportunity to network with other franchisees. Franchises cover a broad range of sectors, from pet delivery and dog grooming businesses to recruitment and training. You can buy a franchise in which you do *all* the actual work *and* focus on the business, or you can buy a management franchise in which you recruit people to do the work leaving you free to focus on the business. The money needed to buy a franchise varies from £5,000 up. The joy of a franchise is that it is tried and tested, and the franchisor has usually done some research in terms of customer demand in your area although you should do your own fact-finding, rather than leaving it to anyone else.

Most newsagents sell copies of magazines such as *Business Franchise* which outlines the possibilities open to you. The British Franchise Association holds exhibitions during the year throughout the UK and it's worth visiting their web site and contacting them for more information. Some banks have advisers who specialise in advising those running a franchise.

Going freelance

If you have a specific skill or are an expert in an area of knowledge, you could put a price on your services and offer yourself as a freelance worker to employers. This option will probably enable you to work from home. It means that you would charge your clients a rate for your services, plus any agreed expenses (such as travel and accommodation if you're working away from home) and possibly VAT depending on how much income your business makes.

Setting up your own business

So you've got a product and service to sell and you want to set up your own business and employ people. You can do this as a sole trader, a partnership, a public liability public partnership, a limited liability company – the best thing is to talk to one or more accountants to decide which suits and your business best.

If you're thinking of buying a franchise (essentially a tried and tested business), this site is for you! There are a whole host of franchises to suit many budgets and interests, including recruitment and training, personal services and IT. *www.british-franchise.org* has details on news, events, seminars, what a franchise is, how to choose a franchise, where to find a franchise and more.

Going portfolio

This means you could be working for one employer or more and setting up your own business as well.

Sorting out practicalities

Doing the admin

If you're planning to set up on your own, you need to think how you're going to cope with all the administration. If you've been used to high powered careers, how will you suddenly feel when faced with paying bills, sending out invoices, doing the filing and books? Can you afford so early on to pay someone to do them? One option is to take on a virtual assistant, rather than hiring someone as a part-time member of staff. You pay by the hour, and you can find one who offers the services you need. Most virtual assistants are experienced personal assistants who have decided to set up on their own. They may work from home or at a centre where a number of businesses are located. Visit www.iava.org.uk for more information.

Keeping track of records

It's vital to keep a thorough track of what is coming into the business and what is going out, even if it's just for the tax man. The HM Revenue and Customs run some excellent workshops to help you start off on the right foot, and they also send you lots of invaluable information so that you can keep on the right side of the Inspector of Taxes. It's much easier to keep good records from day one, rather than trying to sort it all out the day before your tax return is due.

Have you thought about practicalities such as:

	Yes
National insurance and tax	_____
Where you will run your business from	_____
Insurance	_____
Record keeping	_____
Health and safety	_____
Registering for VAT	_____
Writing a business plan	_____
Fire precautions	_____
Employing staff and all that involves	_____

Buildings   _____
Intellectual property   _____
Fair trading   _____
The environment
How IT can help you   _____
Data protection   _____
Licences   _____
The structure your business will have   _____
Official start date!   _____

Help with computers and IT

It's one thing to be employed when you've got some IT whiz about who can help you when the PC crashes. It's another to be on your own. The thing to do is to know who you can turn to for help fast when you've got a problem.

- Don't forget the help desks owned by your internet server and your computer.

- Find out who in your network can help you, for a fee or voluntarily.

- Don't underestimate your ability to sort out a PC problem. Patience is a marvellous thing!

- Be meticulous about running regular virus checks and make sure your virus protection is the best you can get – small firms tend to overlook this. Don't forget to back-up your systems regularly.

Do it now

- What is your vision for your business? By when do you want to achieve it?
- Find out what support is available for you from banks and building societies.
- What can your local Business Link and network organisations do for you?
- Discuss your ideas with your partner. What do they think?

Summary

Make the most of the support available, not just from government agencies but advice from those already running their own businesses.

- Know the pros and cons of running your own business. How do you react to them?

- Don't promise what you cannot deliver.

- Keep in touch with your customers and ask them what you're doing well and what they would like you to introduce.

9

Training, Learning and Boosting Your Skills Base

To be employable, you need to keep learning.

The next few chapters will help you prepare for work. One thing you will find useful will be to undertake some form of training and learning prior to going back to work. This doesn't necessarily mean joining an adult education class; it could mean learning new information, training up in new skills, and updating your knowledge.

Have you considered:

1. What structured learning – if any – you need to achieve your goal?
2. What can you do to show that you're up to speed with what's going on:
   a. in the workplace;
   b. in the sector you want to join;
   c. in the role you want to be in?
3. What do you need to learn if you're going to run your own business?
4. What do you need to do to ensure this learning happens?
5. What are your options to achieve the things you need to do?
6. How committed are you to doing the learning and training you need to ensure success?

7. What support will you need along the way?
8. When do you need to complete the learning by?

First, if the thought of returning to the classroom sounds too horrendous for words, some reassuring news.

What will adult education really be like?

Adult education is constantly changing and will be very different to your school days:

- The way subjects are taught is very different – there's far more use of IT for example.

- Assessment methods have shifted from an emphasis on exams at the end to coursework as you go along.

- In many courses, there is more emphasis on the skills you're taught rather than knowledge and facts.

- In many subjects, you can study at any place, any time, so it's easier than ever before to fit your learning and training into your life. You can learn at home, in work, in libraries, community centres, colleges, even churches and pubs in some areas!

Student attitudes are different, too

Many mature students are terrified at the thought of going back to education. Maybe their school days memories still haunt them. But adult students support each other, and it's a great way to meet people. Classes are much more informal and relaxed and students attend because they want to, for reasons such as those outlined below. Which apply to you?

- Boosting career prospects ☐

- Retraining for a new career ☐

- Training to do something specific ☐

- Going back for the pure fun of it ☐
- Going back to meet people ☐
- Self-development ☐
- To re-boot brain cells before moving on to
  another higher level course ☐
- To re-boot study skills ☐
- Other (specify) ☐

Many colleges run return to study/return to work courses to boost your confidence and study skills. They may enable you to focus on a subject, such as business studies, social science, health studies or science, to prepare for a further course or a particular career path.

As a mature student, entry requirements demanded of you may be different to those sought from younger students, so talk to the college Admissions Office to discuss your background and previous learning prior to enrolling on any pre-course studies.

Training for a job

Whether you're setting up your own business or working for someone else, training is something you should consider. There are huge benefits, not least that tutors should be completely up to date with what's going on in the industry they are training on, and have an extensive network of contacts who may be able to help you when it comes to finding a job. Vocational qualifications (i.e. those related to the workplace) include:

1. Work related qualifications such as Higher National Diplomas or Certificates, and Business and Technology Council (BTEC) courses.
2. Vocational qualifications which may include theory rather than practice, so check carefully before signing up for them to make sure they are what you want. These will give you insight and knowledge into the industry you want to join.

3. National vocational qualifications (NVQs or SVQs in Scotland) which assess your competence to do tasks and skills outlined by very strict criteria.

National vocational qualifications/Scottish vocational qualifications

NVQs/SVQs are based on National Occupational Standards set by leading bodies representing employers. They describe what competent people in particular occupations are expected to be able to do at different levels, so that employers have a very clear idea of what standards and capabilities people have. You should be in employment or involved in relevant voluntary work to acquire an NVQ, but you could pick up some units if your past experience and learning is assessed to be sufficient to make you competent. An assessor will help you work out where you are now and what you can do; and help you outline a programme of on-the-job experience and training to ensure that you are sufficiently competent across the range of tasks you need to be able to do to get the qualification. You can get more information on NVQs at *www.dfes.gov.uk/nvq/*

There are five levels of NVQ:

Level	Type of work
5	Professional, chartered, senior management roles.
4	Technical and junior management occupations.
3	Technician, craft, skilled, supervisory occupations.
2/3	Operative, semi-skilled occupations.
1	Foundation skills. Mostly routine and predictable work.

An NVQ is broken down into a number of units, which in turn break into elements with core activities you need to be able to do at a set standard. In business administration, for example, you would need to show that:

- Requests from your colleagues for help are dealt with promptly and willingly.

- Information is passed on to your colleagues promptly and accurately.

- When you seek assistance, you do so politely.

Your assessor would look at the evidence you have collected to prove you can do each activity – or indeed, watch you in action – to assess whether you have met the required standard.

If you were doing a Level 1 qualification, the sorts of tasks you would have to do would be far simpler than if you were doing a Level 5. Your level would be determined by the sort of job you were already in or the range of experience you already had.

Training for specific jobs

There are also a huge number of practical courses such as City and Guilds and NVQs which will equip you with the skills and knowledge you need to work for a specific career, examples of which are:

Accounting	Business administration
Retail distribution	Hairdressing
Electrical installation	Health and holistic therapies
Plumbing	Tour operator's certificate
Body massage	Teaching English
Nursery nursing	Management
Legal studies	Marketing
Sports coaching	Motor vehicle repairs
Photography	Health care
Counselling	Interior decorating
Financial services	Horticulture
Coaching	Dog grooming
Customer care	Book-keeping
Food preparation	Picture framing
Inn-keeping	Banking

Massage	Returning to learning
Journalism	Creative writing
Antiques	Food hygiene
Furniture restoration	Computing
Printmaking	Animal care
Word processing	Social work

Learning, learning, learning

From an employer's viewpoint, learning shows commitment, energy, enthusiasm and effort. For yourself, it boosts your confidence and authority and your capabilities. There are different ways to learn.

Learning for a purpose

You can learn something new with a specific purpose in mind – book-keeping, for example, so that you can keep the books for your own business if that's what you want to do; even if you don't want to keep the books yourself, you'll need a certain understanding of how they work. This sort of learning could be met by a short course as brief as a morning and will boost your confidence. Many adult education and further education colleges run short courses in many subjects relating to the workplace, such as interview technique and writing a CV.

You can find out more about courses available:

- at your local Business Link and Learning and Skills Council's pages (see Further Information)

- at *www.learndirect.co.uk* – they have courses for individuals and businesses and can put you in touch with the nearest right course for you

- in *Yellow Pages* to find local training and learning providers.

Learning what's changed

If you're going back to a previous career or job, you'll need to know how behaviour and the culture have changed: what's new, what's hot, what's not; have recruitment methods and working conditions changed, and if so how?

As you plot your return to work, have you:

- Talked to colleagues or new contacts at work? ☐

- Taken the trade and professional magazines, available from our newsagent or public libraries? Professional bodies can recommend the right magazines to read. ☐

- Spent time with colleagues at work? ☐

- Read the relevant pages in newspapers and magazines? ☐

- Shadowed people at work for a day or so or more; this means you simply follow them about, keeping a keen eye on what's going on and what's changed since your day? ☐

- Got up-to-date experience by going in and doing? ☐

- Talked to your line-manager or human resources about the training you'll need and worked out and when you're going to do it, if you're going back to your employer? ☐

If you're new to a particular career or sector, an up-to-date knowledge and understanding of the products, services, language and terminology in it will boost your confidence and give you a smoother landing into the workplace when you start.

Learning for the sake of personal development

This is where your academic courses may come in most useful; for example if you want to prove to yourself that yes, you can. Many people choose to do a degree for exactly this reason; perhaps they were frequently told they were useless at school and decide they want to wipe that slate clean and prove to themselves that they're actually very bright indeed.

Do I really need a degree?

The question is: do you need a degree to get to where you want to be? Some professions demand a degree to achieve professional status, but others are more flexible and you may be able to study part-time while you're working in the sector en route to qualifying.

What's on offer?

Courses on offer within higher education include Higher National Diplomas and Certificates, foundation courses, degrees and post-graduate courses. The range of subjects is wide, from the academic (history, English literature, chemistry) to the vocational (information technology, hotel management).

Get hold of a prospectus for full- and part-time courses at your local university to study the full range of courses on offer, and find out whether they run any introductory sessions or open days for mature students who want to go back to higher education. Make the most of mature student advisers who will help you find the right course.

The UCAS site at *www.ucas.com* is invaluable and displays the full range of subjects on offer in the university system. You'll see many which make you think, 'no, that's not for me,' while you respond to others with a 'wow, I've got to find out more about that.' There are many subject combinations now at university, possible through a pick and mix system of units, so you may be able to create a course which is in line with your own interests and career plans.

The UCAS site also has information on student finance and finance for mature students, i.e. people over 21.

Points to ponder

If you're thinking of signing up for a degree, have you considered:

- What are your reasons for entering higher education?

- What difference do you want a degree or course to make to your job prospects? (Find out from the university's careers service what past students have gone on to do after their course.)

- How far will having a degree progress your career in the direction you want it to go?

- Would you be better suited to studying for a degree part time or full time?

- Are you prepared to commit yourself to several years of study?

- How will you fund your course?

- How do you prefer to be assessed? Some courses are assessed more on course-work than exams, for example.

- Do you want to stick to one, two or three subjects?

- Is it your goal to train for a profession?

- Will having a degree guarantee you a job? (And the answer to that is: no, it won't.)

- What will you need to do to apply? And what entry requirements will you have to meet?

The last question is important. Many admissions tutors waive the entry requirements demanded of 18–21 year olds for mature students, if you can show that you have undertaken recent serious academic study and provided that you can prove you've got the necessary knowledge to be successful in the course. This varies from subject to subject: areas such as science and medicine are stricter than those in the humanities. If you don't have the knowledge required for science, mathematics and engineering courses to go straight onto a degree course, you could consider doing a one year Foundation course which will ensure that you do.

You may benefit from studying an Access course, a fast track route for adults wishing to study in higher education, which offers a good grounding in study skills, together with a knowledge of one of several subjects, such as social sciences, media studies, humanities, languages, health, science and sport, dance and music. Again, the UCAS site has information on Access courses, so check them out.

The Credit Accumulation and Transfer System (CATS) enables students to move from one college to another without having to start another course from scratch. This is especially useful if you have to move halfway through your course because your partner has to change location.

Adding up past learning

A system called Accreditation of Prior Learning (APL) enables you to short-cut the full content of the course and study only those parts which are new to you – there's little point in learning again what you already know. A tutor will go through your past studies, experience and knowledge and help you work out how much more you need to do to complete the course you wish to do. Figure 8 shows you the process.

This system is particularly useful with regards to NVQs/SVQs, because they are based on showing that you're competent to do something. You could bring evidence of your competence in voluntary activities you've taken part in, or past work. Many colleges will have an APL tutor so arrange a meeting to discuss where your past learning and study may get you.

Financing study

Costs you could incur may include:

1. The course itself – tuition fees, possibly examination and registration fees.

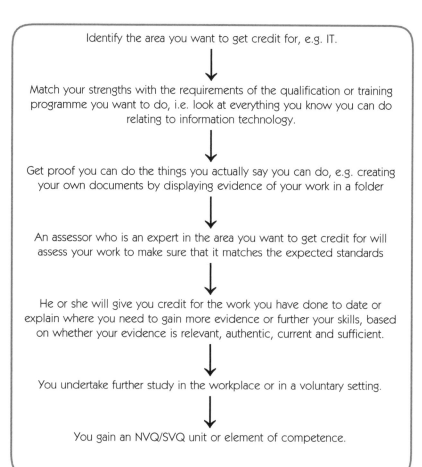

Figure 8: How to get credit for what you can already do

2. Materials – books and any equipment. If you're signing up for a practical course, they may be higher.
3. Transport to get to the course itself.
4. Residential courses plus accommodation, if this forms part of the course.
5. Ad hoc fees for example to join a professional body if you're looking to boost your career prospects.

Find out whether there will be any other expenses or fees so that you don't have any nasty surprises. Talk to your provider's Finance Office. There may be concessionary fees to students who are out of work, self-employed or retired; they will have details of different grants and loans available. They should also know about any tax relief you might be eligible for as a result of signing up for the course, and if you choose to take out a Career Development Loan or any other such help, they will be able to help you complete any forms required if you get stuck.

So where's the money going to come from to pay for courses?

It's important to do your homework and really delve into sources of finance for any courses you want to do.

Learning and Skills Councils

Your county may be offering grants, loans or a whole host of financial assistance to help you in training and learning, so why not find out what your local county is doing to help you? Every county is different in terms of what's on offer, but they all want to maximise learning and training opportunities for all those living in the area. Visit *www.lsc.gov.uk* for more information on Learning and Skills Councils or your council's web site to find out more.

Access or hardship funds

Many training providers have access or hardship funds to help students when the going gets really tough. The finance office will have details. Study their web sites to see if you can find out about possible funding – don't just assume there are no other ways forward. Your local college, for example, may be working with local partners such as colleges and universities to boost skills in a particular sector or area. Call or visit the institution's web site to find out.

Career Development Loans

These allow you to borrow anywhere between £300 and £8,000 to spend on two years of learning and up to one year's practical work experience if it forms part of your chosen course. Visit *www.lifelonglearning.co.uk* for more information.

Juggling life and study

We all have our own commitments in life and you need to identify a system whereby you can study, learn and train at times to suit you. Find a time when your brain power and motivation works best and you're least likely to be disturbed.

Training and learning providers try to make life easy for you by offering a range of facilities, including:

- A library and flexible learning centre, where you can work and research.
- Tours of the college facilities at the start of your course.
- Childcare provision – spaces may be limited so enquire early.
- Courses during the day (some are timed to fit in with school hours), evening, even weekends.
- Email and/or personal tutor support.
- Return to study courses – invaluable if you haven't studied for a long time, as they are designed to boost your study skills and capabilities.

Tutors recognise that it's not easy being an adult student, as you try to fit your studies in with the responsibilities of adulthood. Alert them to problems sooner rather than later and ask for help as soon as you need it, rather than letting worries build up.

What if the course isn't right for me?

Some people start a course and find that it's simply at the wrong level. If this happens to you, talk to your tutor and see if you can move to a more appropriate class.

Case study: Nicola studying French

'I enrolled for French but I knew I was struggling by week two! I spoke to my tutor and the Adult Registration team. The lady I spoke to in Adult Registration listened carefully and said, "Well, the important thing is that you enjoy your studies – we must find you another course." I swapped to a lower level, where I'm coping better and enjoying myself.'

Don't forget: you can study at home

There are lots of distance learning courses available from all kinds of training providers, including universities and colleges. The Open University (see Useful Addresses) offers a wide range of courses from arts and humanities to health and social welfare, and from business and management to the environment. It has regional centres around the UK which provide advice and guidance to prospective students.

The Association of British Correspondence Courses (see Useful Addresses) will send you a list of approved organisations. The National Extension College is one example of a major provider of distance-learning courses, many of which are career related. You start when you like, and receive your course material after you have signed up. You work at your pace, sending in assignments for marking and receiving comments back from your own personal tutor. Colleges should provide back up and support, and be happy to put you in touch with students who have studied the course you're considering taking so that you can get their point of view on the student support, course materials and so forth.

Know why you're studying, learning or training and your motivation will rocket!

Become an e-learner

Why not become an e-learner? You can do so on an informal basis by surfing the Internet to boost your knowledge on subjects you particularly want to know about. For example, if you searched the Internet for information on handling teenagers, then you would be an informal learner. Alternatively, you can study more structured courses on-line, such as those provided by Learndirect.

The advantage of being an e-learner is that you can really learn at your own pace when it suits you. But it can be impersonal and lonely, and you may prefer a learning option which is more social and gets you out of the house.

Taking a refresher course

Many professions and colleges now run refresher courses for people seeking to return to work in their sectors. Some sectors are better at this than others; the NHS for example and engineering sectors (for women) are two shining examples. If you're planning on going back to the sector you were in before:

1. Check with your professional or trade body what is available.
2. Contact local colleges in your area and go through to the most relevant department.
3. Visit the web sites for employers and private training providers in the sector too – they may offer their own refresher courses.

Have you found out:

- Will you have to pay for return to work training? ☐
- Is financial support available for refresher courses? ☐
- How will the course boost your chances of landing a job? ☐
- What flexibility will there be in the time you study? ☐

- How much academic content will there be and how well are you personally prepared for that? ☐

- What support is available while you are studying? And what support is offered once you've gone back? ☐

- What skills will the course teach you that will enable you to hit the ground running? ☐

- Will it include a stint of work experience out in the field? ☐

- What do you need to do to apply? ☐

Some large employers run their own 'return to work' courses, so check with yours if you're going back to see if they do.

General refresher courses are on offer too!

Many colleges and training providers offer generalist courses designed to help you get your toe into the water. These can be particularly useful if you want to take a new look at your career.

> Be persistent. Dig about to find refresher courses in your sector and region and make the most of them.

Do it now

- Think about how you learn best. By doing? Watching others and then doing it yourself? Studying the theory and then putting that into practice? In a classroom?
- Where do you want to learn? At a class in your area? Do you want to move away and start afresh through study? On-line?
- Find the courses on offer in your area and find out what you need to do to apply and fund your studies.

Summary

Training and learning are both lifelong skills today so it's important to:

- Keep track of what's on offer in your area that's relevant to you, your career and personal aspirations and the sector you want to work in.
- Be sure of how you like to learn so that you can find the learning conditions that suit you best.
- Remember you can learn in many different ways – the key is to keep learning.

10

Confidence and Skills Boosters

❝If you think you can or think you can't, you're right.❞

Henry Ford

This chapter is all about boosting your chances of success in returning to work in the role you want. Employers are amazingly receptive to helping people who help themselves, and activities such as voluntary work and work experience will enhance your knowledge and confidence and your understanding of how the workplace has changed.

Assess where you are now and what you need to make this return to work happen.

1. What exactly do I need to do to boost my chances of success?
2. How will this activity move me closer to returning to work?
3. What specifically do I need to get out of them to make them effective?
4. What do I need to do to make them happen?
5. When am I going to do it?
6. Whose support will I need and when and how am I going to get that support?

Getting work experience

If you haven't been in paid employment for a long time, dip your toe in the water and get some work experience. You can get your hands dirty and get stuck in and active by doing (work experience) or watch what someone else doing the job is doing as their shadow (work shadowing). You can find out what's happening in the sector and talk to people first hand about it. They will tell you the pros and cons of it and – importantly – how to get a foot in the door.

Work experience expected?

If you want to enter a very competitive area, such as media, then relevant work experience is a must. Even that may be difficult to get, so make good use of your networks to get the help you need. Many courses offer a period in real live work situations so that you can put into practice all that theory. This provides an opportunity to get back into touch with the workplace, but also to network with employers and show what you can do for them.

Finding work experience

Employers won't be surprised by requests for work experience or work shadowing. They are being asked to provide increasing numbers of such opportunities by schools, colleges and universities, private training and career companies and government run employment and training programmes. If you want to acquire experience, why not get in touch with employers directly and ask if you can have a couple of days with them. If you have special circumstances, get help and support from those who know you in an official capacity.

Making the most of voluntary work

Voluntary work is a great way to boost your confidence and get back into a work situation, where you're working with a group of people towards a common goal and acquiring experience. Employers like to see voluntary work on a CV; it tells them you're motivated, and you can talk about the team working skills you've developed, your customer service abilities and flexible approach.

> Voluntary work can play an invaluable role in your return to work. It can open up avenues and careers in organisations you'd never thought of working for.

Case Study: Susannah becomes a teaching assistant

'I'd had a short break from my sales job and the head teacher at my son's school asked if I'd like to help the kids with behavioural problems for a month. I loved it, but at the end, I went back to my sales job. Three years later, the head called me and explained she was recruiting a teaching assistant in the same unit and she wondered if I was interested. I jumped at it! My earlier voluntary efforts had enabled me to put a foot in the door and prove myself, not just to me but to the school, too.'

How can voluntary work help you?

Voluntary work will help if you want to:

- Prove that you're interested in the line of work you want to enter.
- Show that you've got the ability to relate to the people you'd be dealing with, such as the elderly, people with disabilities, or children.
- Expand your skills base into areas where you want to work.
- Acquire a passion for something.
- Make a difference to a cause that's important to you.
- Build up a clear idea of the skills you can offer an employer.
- Practise working in a team environment with people you don't know.
- Boost your confidence.

- Increase your network of contacts.

- Get back into the routine and discipline of work, and practise handling home emergencies and problems.

- Show what you can do to yourself and an employer.

- Show an employer you have motivation and initiative.

Finding voluntary work

The opportunities to do voluntary work are fantastic and growing, so you should find something which relates to your interests and skills in the UK, or even abroad. You could approach local charities, who may advertise in the local paper or library, or whom you can find through your telephone book or the Internet. Equally, you could turn to organisations such as the National Centre for Volunteering or TimeBank, which can match your skills and interests to opportunities in your area.

Skills you could put into practice include:

- counselling
- advising
- informing
- promoting
- selling
- befriending
- market research
- interviewing
- administering
- record keeping
- conserving
- driving
- fund-raising
- recruiting
- mentoring
- project managing
- visiting
- programming
- presenting
- home checking

> Go for something that really interests you, that you care about and want to contribute to. Your experience will be far more enjoyable and meaningful.

If you're asked what you want to do, don't just say anything! This is your chance to develop skills you really want to use in work. Some organisations will provide training, and certainly, that and any experience you acquire can go some way towards National Vocational Qualifications, if you decide to study for them.

Any vacancies going?

The voluntary sector is really sharpening up its act and becoming far more businesslike which means that any experience you've acquired in the private sector before taking your break could be of interest to them. Most charities have web sites with details of any career opportunities. Plot the skills and experience you're acquiring in your voluntary work and sell it to employers on your CV and at an interview.

Finally, consider:

- What you've contributed to the overall effort and explain how you fitted in with the other members of your team.
- What difference you made.
- What relationship you built up with the rest of the team.
- How you overcame problems, challenges and change.

> Market your voluntary efforts on your CV as if you were describing a job. Talk about your skills, experience and achievements.

As a result of your voluntary work, your CV might include something like this:

> 200X–200Y Receptionist at Stateside Hostel two afternoons a week
>
> - Assisted on reception at the hostel and made visitors feel welcome; explained the role of the hostel and answered incoming queries; kept diaries for three social workers.
> - Enjoyed working in a team and with a wide variety of customers; the role frequently demanded patience, firmness, tact and an ability to calm down aggressive people.

The employer knows that once you've been shown how their office systems work, you can function straightaway because you know how to welcome people, you enjoy teamwork and you have organising skills.

When applying for a job as a retail assistant in a store, Angela wrote:

> 200X Worked in St Claire's School Shop Selling Second Hand Uniforms
>
> - ran shop with two women one afternoon a week
> - responsible for handling money (cash, cheque and credit card transactions)
> - promoted shop within the school at a wide variety of functions
> - frequently worked rapidly under pressure
> - maintained shop records, shop made a profit of £2,500, an increase of 15% on 200Y
> - assisted in the production of Annual Report to the PTA

This CV shows a variety of skills – all gained through voluntary efforts. What's more, when Angela wanted to gain more qualifications and when she visited her local college, she discovered she could get credit for much of the work she had done voluntarily towards a National Vocational Qualification in Customer Services and Business Administration. All she had to do was to provide the evidence.

Accessing government help

To make the most of the human resources available, the government has many programmes designed to help people back into work. If you've tried one of these already and it didn't work for you, ask yourself why. Try again, and use different strategies to ensure success. In the UK, Regional Development Agencies and Learning and Skills Councils are working to ensure that local employers have the people with the right skills they need to ensure economic success. The good news for you is that this means there will be more opportunities in employment, training and education. You will need to see if there are any eligibility requirements.

Some government-run training schemes offer a chance to get out in the workplace and see how you get on. The best outcome is that you get on very well, and that the employer you're with offers you paid work. You each have a chance to see how you get on with the other and with the work to be done.

Additionally, there are a number of programmes such as apprenticeships, the New Deal scheme and others, which give adults the chance to return to work, although you may need to meet certain criteria to be accepted on them. There will also be a number of schemes to help you set up your own business, if that's what you want. Your local Jobcentre Plus (gradually being introduced to replace Jobcentres) will have details of these and will also be able to tell you how joining them may affect any benefits you receive.

Most training programmes offer you elements such as:

- Short term training to give you the skills you need to find work or to do a specific job.

- Job placements, which give you an introduction to an employer and a job; this could lead to permanent work.

- Training leading to National Vocational Qualifications, which show how competent you are at a specific job.

These programmes may be particularly useful if you're very nervous about going back to work or if you have special barriers to overcome, and you should receive lots of support and help from your adviser and the employer. Some programmes and initiatives target specific groups, such as New Deal 50 Plus, New Deal 25 Plus and the New Deal for Disabled People. Programmes such as these may entitle you to training grants and possible financial help with clothes or fares for interviews. Check with your local Jobcentre Plus how they might affect your benefits.

My area suffers from high unemployment

Find out what your local Learning and Skills Council (see Useful Addresses) is doing to create jobs and provide training. There's a huge amount of funding available to regenerate certain areas in the UK, by creating new jobs and employment parks, and your region could be one of them. Your willingness to learn new skills and try something different will be crucial to your success. Hankering after the way things used to be isn't going to help you bring a salary in and secure a job for the future. You could also consider working from home for employers anywhere in the world on your PC via the Internet.

Enlisting support

There are many networks and groups to help people with particular needs return to work. Tap into their experience and expertise. They will have invaluable advice and practical suggestions to make. Figure 9 gives an example of the variety of support groups in society, all of whom have support networks.

Even if you don't think you need any additional help, why not tap into networks relevant to you and your situation? Many groups have information and advice on:

- possible benefits you might be eligible for
- support available
- advice on tackling particular issues
- laws, regulations and your rights at work
- fact sheets
- how to contact others in a similar situation – it can help to know you're not alone
- projects and initiatives in your area
- links to other helpful web sites
- their own recruitment page
- any conferences they are running
- practical advice and tips on returning to work and managing your life once you're back

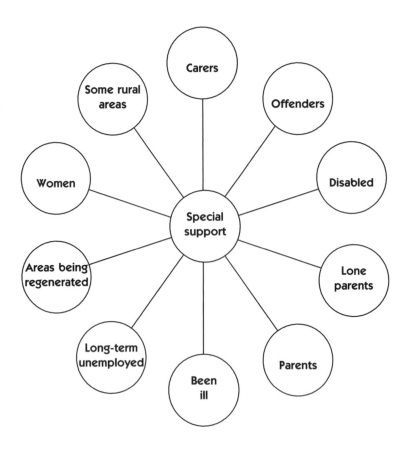

Figure 9. Examples of support networks

- useful publications
- news and campaigns they are running

Some support organisations such as Carers UK have developed learning and training programmes that you can do at home which take into account skills and knowledge you've been using while you've been out of the workplace.

Trying and testing first

There's an old saying: look before you leap. If you're to have a happy career and do well at work, you need information about the workplace and yourself – and how the two marry up together – before you start working again. There are plenty of ways to get started and lots of help available, so make the most of the opportunities to do so. Better to do your research and follow the right track than jump on the wrong train. This is especially the case if you're moving in a new direction – any potential employer will want proof that you've done your research and you're sure your new career is right for you.

Trying new things

When was the last time you tried something new? How did you cope? What did that experience teach you about yourself? How can you use that knowledge about yourself now?

Taking it step by step

Remember that your return to work is directed by you at your own pace. It requires continual effort and you will receive knock-backs. The key is to keep trying. Persistence pays off.

Knowing what makes an organisation tick

Exercise

Business or commercial awareness will stand you in good stead today. Take any two businesses which spring to mind – one should be a national or global outfit, the other a local one. Find out as much as you can in answer to the following questions:

- What is the organisation's main goal?
- What are their strengths and weaknesses
- What pressures are they under?

- Who decides what products they should market and sell, and the price they should be sold at?
- What threats do they face? What opportunities have they to expand?
- What do they do that is most effective?
- What could they do better?
- What legislation exists in terms of the way they recruit and fire staff?
- What challenges do they face?
- What tensions and power struggles might there be internally?
- Where do they get their information from about their customers and the economy?
- What changes are taking place in the world which will affect the way they operate and what their clients want?

Read what you can in newspaper business pages and any articles relevant to sectors which interest you to find out what is going on. Talk to people at work – what do they think is happening to their organisation and to the business world? Create a questioning approach.

Going back to your old company

If you're headed back to a past employer, renew contact with them if you haven't been in touch with them while you've been out of the workplace.

Find out from their human resources department what they need from you and what is on offer to help you start back. Talk to your line-manager about returning to work:

- Do they offer internal refresher courses or return to work days?

- What support is available, such as employee assisted services and counselling?

- If you've been ill, can your hours be reduced or changed so that you can travel out of rush hours?

- What will happen to any benefits you've been receiving?

- Put a return to work plan together to help make the process easier so that each of you know what is expected of the other.

- Go in for a coffee with your colleagues or meet them for lunch.

- Can you start off by working from home?

- What return to work policies does the company have, if any?

- What can you start receiving at home to prepare you for your return, e.g. emails, newsletters, phone calls...?

- Can you go in for team meetings just to get back into the thick of things slowly?

At the same time, get in touch with any relevant support groups outside of work so that you can be sure of your rights when you go back. If you're recovering from an illness, talk to your doctor or consultant about how you might feel for a while – you may feel very exhausted, for example, but want to return to work to have some normality in your life.

Companies handle people returning to work after time out in different ways and some are better than others at handling it. Do your bit by finding out what you can, but remember to look forward and that health comes first! Better to do little well than try to do too much and have a relapse.

Do it now

- Find out what help and support is on offer in your area for returners to work.
- Identify employers you could approach for work experience.
- Look back at any voluntary work you've done. Analyse it for the skills and experience you acquired.
- Identify opportunities for voluntary work in your area.
- Follow them up and become a volunteer for a couple of afternoons or mornings a week while you're plotting your return to work.

 **Summary**

Voluntary efforts and work experience offer huge opportunities to build your confidence, increase your network and develop your skills.

- They are particularly useful if you haven't worked for ages or at all, and you want some extra support.
- You will be astounded at how much you can learn from them.
- Take any chance you can get to be adventurous and make contact with people who work in the sectors which interest you most.

11

Your Job-Hunting Tool Kit

❝Get ready! The process of landing a job could be really fast!❞

It's easy to assume that you're ready to go out and start looking for work or starting up your own business. Your mind may be ready, but there are several tools you should have ready if you're to go out there and impress!

Contact me!

However you plan to job hunt, a key ingredient of success is to have tools at your disposal with which prospective employers can contact you *fast*. If you're planning to set up your own business, this is equally the case.

Have you:

Got a mobile phone?   Yes/No
Leave your name on it and ask callers to leave a message.
Check it regularly for messages.

Got a private email address? Yes/No

This is invaluable if you want to connect. Check it regularly and create a signature for business purposes with your contact details to include name, address, phone number and mobile. You can use a computer at your local library to set up an email address and receive email.

Take as much care when putting an email together as you would if you were writing a letter on paper. Consider what image your email will create of you if you send it to someone you've never met before. Be brief and to the point, and leave the text/teen speak 'C U' to your teenagers.

Got a sensible answer phone at home? Yes/No

If you expect calls from anyone who could make an impact on your career, warn those you live with so that they can pick up the phone to callers and respond appropriately with polite and professional tones. This is particularly the case if you've got children at home. It's excellent training for them.

Updated your contacts regularly? Yes/No

Networking is key to successful job hunting, so review all your contacts (private and work) and get in touch with those you think may be able to help you every few months or so.

Updating your image

Go and watch people who work for the sort of company you'd love to work for leave their place of work. What do they look like? Does everyone wear a business suit or is the dress less formal than that? Have the men all got short hair cuts, or doesn't that appear to matter? Do jeans and t-shirts appear to be a part of the make-up, or are those non-existent? Are the women carefully made-up and stylish, with polished nails and high heels? What is the average age of those leaving the workplace? Are people all young, or does there appear to be a good mixture of ages? Image covers everything from appearance (top to toe) to the way you talk, from your posture, to the language you use.

Take a good hard, honest look at yourself in a full length mirror. Put on the clothes you intend to wear for interview and then for work when you go back. For each outfit ask yourself:

1. Do you need a hair cut? Would something totally different transform the way you look and think about yourself and give you a new-found confidence? Would a change in hair colour give you a younger look, if you think that's needed?
2. What can you do to sharpen up your image? Do you need to do some exercise or give up the booze for a bit to give you a more focused look? Do you look energetic and enthusiastic, or as though you spend all day watching television?
3. What is your posture like? Do you slouch through laziness or hold yourself upright in a relaxed way? Ask yourself this when you're sitting down, too. Do you fidget with your hands and play with anything you can get hold of?
4. What does your image say about you to the industry you want to work in, to a future employer, and to potential customers or clients?
5. What image does the industry you want to work in seek to portray to its customers and clients? What is important about that image to them?
6. Do you look as though you would fit into the environment and culture you want to work in or stand out like a sore thumb?

If you're confident you look your best on the outside, you'll feel much better inside.

Pulling your resources together

Get in with a support group

Get together with three or four friends or new mates, each with a goal, not necessarily relating to returning to work. Support and motivate each other, and celebrate together as you all progress on your journey.

Join up with positive, go-getting types who talk about what they want, not those who moan and blame others when things go wrong. Negative people will drain you of the energy you need and steer your focus in the direction of failure and excuses rather than success and action. If you only know negative people, go out and find some new positive people.

Live as if you're back at work

Live daily life as if you were working to get an idea of how things will pan out. For example:

- How will you cope if the kids or your mother are sick or if the cat needs taking to the vet urgently?

- What is the public transport like from your home to the areas you want to work in and what will it cost? Have you tried taking it first thing in the morning and what sorts of problems can you expect? How will you cope with those?

- What will you do for lunch and mid-morning and afternoon snacks? Get into the habit of preparing healthy food the night before, and it will be easier to look after yourself and your money when you start work again.

- What are you going to wear when you go back?

- How will you handle household chores and what you can you do now to start making life easier for yourself? Do you need to hire a cleaner? Can you delegate to the children and prepare them for their new found responsibilities in the home before you go back, so they are trained up when you go back?

Get positive

Stay clear of negative news and views; it's amazing how much the press focuses on it, but then bad news sells. Delete it from your brain when you can while you're looking for work.

- Listen to the language of successful people carefully. How positive are they? How negative?

- Monitor your own language for a week. How negative are you in daily life? What can you do to make yourself talk more positively and with greater belief in yourself?

Exercise is a great way to help you stay positive. Is there a walkers' or runners' group you can join? Can you go cycling or swimming two or three times a week, or take part in Pilates, five-a-side football or horse-riding? Apart from anything else, you'll continually extend your network and meet people who may provide the lead to that perfect job.

Statistics about people returning to work don't help either. They relate to people in their situation, not you in yours. Once you consider yourself to be a statistic, you might as well jump on the unemployed pile. You're better than a statistic. You're you, an individual in a unique situation with special talents and skills and your own aspirations, needs, values and plans.

Track and celebrate your progress

How much further are you moving towards your goal every day? Celebrate when you send your CV off for that first time, when you get called for an interview, after the interview is over, when you've got that job! Remind yourself of how far you've come since you started plotting your return to work and your confidence will continue to grow.

Are you eligible for any benefits?

Financial help is available to help you make the transition between claiming benefits and returning to work. These come in the form of various grants and bonuses, benefits and funds. Such as:

- Job Grant
- Extended Housing Benefit and Council Tax Benefit

- Benefits for Loan Parents
- Adviser Discretion Fund
- Child Tax Credit
- Working Tax Credit
- In Work Emergencies Fund.

Talk to your local Jobcentre Plus to find out what benefits you may be eligible for and how they may affect any others you currently receive.

Making the most of opportunities to prepare

Your preparation for work should be on-going. Whether you're starting up your own business or planning to work for someone else, consider actions you can take to enhance your understanding of the world you want to work in. This could mean attending networking events in your area put on by your sector; reading trade magazines and going to trade shows; finding out about new products and services. Look closely at the culture: what goes, what doesn't, learn 'the lingo', what are the trends and challenges ahead.

Boost your chances of success

There are plenty of things you need to be doing to find that right role for you if you're returning to work but looking for a new employer.

On a weekly basis you should be:

- completing application forms ☐
- writing your CV ☐
- attending interviews ☐
- researching employers ☐

- keeping in touch with your agency, if you've registered with one ☐

- learning new skills ☐

- updating yourself ☐

- networking ☐

- attending locally run courses in improving your interview technique ☐

- reading email alerts from job sites ☐

- checking Internet sites for new vacancies ☐

These are just some suggestions.

Why not ask if you can spend some time with a company?

If you're going to hit the ground running and really show enthusiasm, why not approach a company you'd like to work for, or at the very least one in your chosen field, and ask if you can help out for a couple of days or more a week? The benefits of doing this are:

- You boost your confidence by handling work-related situations.

- You're learning new skills.

- You're proving what you can do.

- You could ask the employer for a reference.

- You could get new leads: *We're not taking anyone on, but I'll have a word with Geoff Smith down the road at L and G Woods. I've got a feeling he may be looking to take someone on...*

- You're showing your motivation and commitment.

- It will give you something to talk about at future interviews.

- It will show you first hand what's changed in the workplace.

Highlighting your assets

Remind yourself of the assets you've got. Practise your answers to:

- *Tell me about yourself.*
- *Tell me what you've been doing in your time away from work.*
- *Why should we hire you?*

Start putting a CV together, pulling all the background from your life history that will be relevant to the career you want. Now is an excellent time to consider how you can sell the skills you've acquired in your break to the benefit of potential employers and, if you're changing career totally, to think how a fresh approach will benefit your new employer. What will be particularly relevant? How can you describe your time out? What skills has that given you? Why are you returning to work now? Start thinking about answers to inevitable questions and also consider questions you will want answered. If you're starting your own business, what can you show you have in your background that will enhance your success? Are there any gaps you should be filling which you can do now, while you're looking for work?

Identify your achievements

- What have you achieved during your break?
- What projects have you undertaken?
- What have you learnt?
- What skills have you developed as a result of these achievements and projects? How can you demonstrate that you have these skills? Which examples could you use?
- How can you show that your break has developed your transferable skills?
- What have you done to plan your return to work? (This shows that you are taking your move seriously and know that the move you're making is the right one for you.)

Turning negatives into positives

Now is a good time to start turning any negatives into positives so that you're prepared to cover any sticky questions you may be asked. We all make mistakes in life – employers too – and the main thing is that you can show an employer that you've learnt from yours and have moved on from them. If there are gaps in your life which you'd rather not be open about, think carefully about how you're going to cover them. If you were detained at Her Majesty's pleasure, for example, be honest and open. Show that you've turned over a new leaf. If you've had time out to raise a family, say so. Employers dislike gaps in CVs – they immediately wonder what the owner is trying to hide.

Be persistent

It can take a while to find the role you want with the company you want to work for. And if you're setting up your own business, that may take time too. Remember that those who persist, succeed. Those who give up, fail. If you want to find a job, you need to persist until you get one. That sounds obvious, but it's easy to forget!

Be clear in your own mind about what will work for you

Finally, remind yourself of what you need for a sane and sensible work–life balance. If you can only work 20 hours a week because you need the rest of the time free for something you need to take care of – or someone – be prepared to say so. If you see that perfect job advertised, and it's full time and you can only do half the hours required, consider whether you can find someone to job share with you, or whether you could work part time from home and part time in the office. But be prepared to be honest with potential employers. If you cannot travel for the job, for example, say so.

Do it now

- Prepare your job-hunting kit. If the phone rang tomorrow morning, asking you to come in for an interview in the afternoon, would you be ready?
- If a company called you to interview you over the telephone, would you be ready to answer their questions?
- Have you got everything to hand? Certificates, any documentation you might need to bring in?
- Do messages you leave on your home and mobile phones give the right impression of someone who is professional and motivated? Listen and see. Change them if you need to.
- Talk to as many people as you can who've gone back to work. How did they do it? What challenges did they face and what would their advice be to you?

Summary

As you prepare to go out and secure a role, you need to make sure you're properly prepared.

- Be organised so that you don't waste time and energy panicking when the phone goes.

- Keep a pen and paper by the phone ready to take notes.

- Follow up on contacts you make by phoning or emailing people to touch base with them and let them know how you're getting on.

12

Marketing and Promotion

6The goal of a CV is to entice an employer to such an extent that they want to meet you.9

It's time to market and sell your skills, achievements, competences, potential contribution and assets, as any company would to potential customers and promote those to prospective employers. The CV is the standard tool for doing just that. You need to build a bridge between where you are now, and where you want to be.

To sell yourself effectively, you must know what you have to offer to potential employers. Similarly, if you're setting up your own business, you need to know what you can offer your business and potential customers. To be confident and convincing in selling yourself, you need evidence of your skills, abilities, achievements.

If you're applying on spec, an employer may keep your CV in case their staff needs change: you could fulfil some gap they have and add value to the team. Follow up your CV with a phone call to see if you can contact them again in a few months' time.

What do CVs include?

The main purpose behind a CV is to attract an employer's interest in you to such an extent that they want to meet you and talk further. A

CV will show an employer what you're capable of and what you can contribute, while recent study gives an idea of your potential. Your CV should show where you're heading, and, if you've done your research properly and present yourself well, you should be able to show that your values match those of the organisation you're applying to.

A typical CV normally includes the following sections:

- Contact details.
- A short personal statement of about 25–40 words about the future role you're looking for.
- Relevant past experience.
- Qualifications.
- Details of any organisations you belong to, including details of any posts you hold and your achievements within that role.
- Leisure activities and hobbies.

Writing a winning CV

It takes the average employer a couple of minutes to read and assess a CV, and that's assuming yours gets to the 'to be read' pile. Essential key elements of a successful CV are that it is:

- Accurate.
- Well laid out and easy to read, enabling the reader to make notes in the left and right margins.
- Honest – most employers will check out what you've written.
- Concise – use bullet points rather than paragraphs.
- Relevant to what you want to do.
- No more than 2 pages.
- Without any spelling or grammatical errors at all.
- On clean fresh A4 paper without décor.

Preparing to write your CV

Before you start writing, take some time to stop and think and plan. This preparation is key. Questions to ask yourself include:

1. What job or career move do you want next? What do you want the role to involve?
2. Whose attention do you need to attract?
3. What do you want to show them?
4. What information do they most need to know about you?
5. What message do you want to portray about yourself?
6. If you are responding to an advert, what specifically is the employer looking for (Chapter 14 will help you with that).
7. What can you do to boost your chances of success?

Figure 10 (p. 154) shows you a process to follow.

Show an employer what you can do

It's important to give potential employers a clear idea of what you can do and want to do. Josephine Ladel is applying for a PA job in a leisure centre. Her first shot at writing her CV tells the employer very little, as Figure 11 (p. 155) shows. There is too much information about her previous educational qualifications and not enough about the skills she used in her previous career which were relevant to posts she was applying for. Employers are not interested in your children. Josephine has a more successful attempt in Figure 12 (pp. 156–7).

 **Analysing a CV**

Let's go through her CV in Figure 12 section by section.

Contact details

Josephine has put her details – name, address, home and mobile number and email address – in the centre of the page at the top for fast reference. There is no need to put CV at the top.

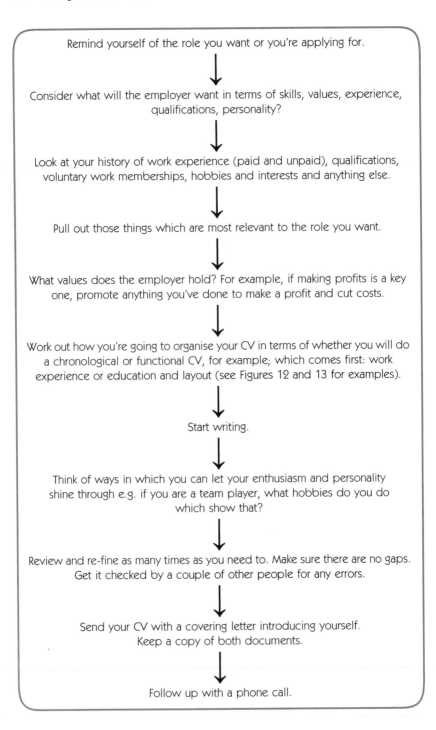

Figure 10: Writing a CV

Mrs Josephine Ladel
Soupson Cottage
Soup Lane
Littletown
(0011 111111)

1986–2006   Raised my family of three children. The boys are now 18, 16
             and 14.

1983–1986   Joe Ellen & Co Ltd, Littletown
             Secretary to Managing Director

1981–1983   Joe Ellen & Co Ltd, Littledown
             Secretary to Personnel Manager

Educational Qualifications

1980–1981   Secretarial College

1975–1980   Littletown Girls School, 8 O levels:

             Cookery – A
             Needlework - A
             French – C
             English - C
             Maths – C
             History C
             Biology – C
             Art – C

Hobbies and Interests

Member of the PTA
Tennis, badminton, going to the cinema on a Friday night

Figure 11: A CV which says little about the applicant

Mrs Josephine Ladel
Soupson Cottage
Soup Lane
Littletown
(Home: 0011 111111; Mob: 07800 321 321)
jladel@spoon.com

Career Aspirations
Seeking role within the leisure sector managing a small team of assistants while supporting the management and broadening my managerial and PA experience.

Work Experience
1986–2006   Career Break: Managed my family and home

- Developing skills in managing, communicating, organising, negotiating, self-management, motivating and caring for others;
- Responsible for financial and administrative aspects of the house, including budgeting and cost cutting, house maintenance, insurance and utilities.

1983–1986   Joe Ellen & Co Ltd, Littletown, Publishing Company of 100 staff
Promoted to PA to Managing Director

- Managed team of 6 secretaries, with responsibility for recruitment, induction and training, organising holiday and sick cover in co-operation with Personnel Department.
- Organised 15 corporate events, including annual Christmas Party for 250 people.
- Responsible for sending out mail shots to 1,000 prospective customers and recording update on database.
- Organised quarterly board meetings, including preparation of confidential documents and minute taking.

1981–1983   Joe Ellen & Co Ltd, Littletown
Secretary to Personnel Manager

- Responsible for smooth running of interviews: arranged whole process with candidates and interviewers.
- Verified qualifications with educational institutions and employers.
- Maintained record system.
- Audio typing (45 words per minute), photocopying, making refreshments.

Figure 12. A CV which sells an applicant.

Educational Qualifications
1980–1981   St Goldsmiths Further Education College
             Secretarial Course

Acquired qualifications in audio typing (40wpm), shorthand (100wpm) and studied secretarial duties.

1975–1980   Littletown Girls School

             8 O level passes, including Mathematics, English and French.

Additional Skills
- Computer literate: Word, Excel, Powerpoint all advanced. Currently learning Publisher;
- A level French through night classes in 2002-2004;
- Clean driving licence plus qualified to drive mini bus;
- First aid Qualification with St John's Ambulance Brigade.

Hobbies and Interests
Parent Teacher Association, Littletown Secondary School Secretary (2001-present), Committee Member and Secretary. Send out agendas, minute-taking, ensure actions are followed up in time for meetings, liaise with Chair, handle correspondence.

Tennis, member of local tennis club committee; organised sponsored tennis tournament to raise £8,000 towards new club house. 80 players participated over long weekend. Played for the club in second league.

Badminton: responsible for refreshment rota every Friday in 2003-2004 winter season. Organised members to serve teas, bake cakes, for 40 people.

Films, particularly historical in nature.

Other points of interest
Marital status: Married
Nationality: British
Date of Birth: 9 June 1964
References available upon request

Figure 12. (continued).

Career aspirations

It's a useful idea to put a short 30–40 word statement about your career aspirations at the top as a sort of personal profile.

Past work experience

An employer is only interested in what is relevant to them. Josephine has made no apology for taking time out – she has simply explained what she has been doing and given the employer an idea of the skills she has developed which will be useful to him. The rest of her CV has been written in such as a way as to highlight further skills she has as a result of taking on positions of responsibility outside the home such as projects (fund raising for the tennis club), routine tasks (badminton refreshments) and learning (night classes).

For each role you have had, select and emphasis those skills and achievements which are most relevant to the post you now want. If Josephine was applying for a role where organising meetings was more important, for example, she would have emphasised that more. As it is, the activities Josephine has outlined have enabled her to develop skills in managing, organising and ensuring things run smoothly and getting people on board which will be invaluable to her in the next role she wants. By including the simpler tasks, she has shown she can muck in and that she understands the importance of more junior roles.

Educational qualifications

Demonstrate any recent learning you have done to prove you are able and willing to learn. Most employers cannot keep up with changes in education so describe your qualifications in such a way that an employer can see what you can do for him or her. Don't leave them guessing or wondering. '2002–4 National Vocational Qualification Level II, Information Technology' won't mean much but the same qualification outlined as follows will give greater clarity:

2002–2004 National Vocational Qualification Level II, Information Technology

- Expert at keying into a computer.
- Experienced in using spreadsheets.
- Composed range of business correspondence.
- Currently learning to use Powerpoint.

Put in any current studies you're taking – you can always put 'Results due in June 2006' or 'to be completed in June 2006' after the qualification you are studying for.

Similarly for languages, be specific about what you can do and be honest. Your employer will probably test your skills at interview.

2005-2006   French GCSE taken at Moorstown College of Further Education
Able to converse in French and write simple business letters. Result due June 2006.

Josephine has chosen to list her computer skills under 'additional skills'. You will need to play with your CV and see where you think things like this fit best.

Spare time activities

These might include leisure interests and hobbies, voluntary efforts or points of interest which might be relevant, such as professional association memberships, clubs or societies. Anything that shows an employer you're a well rounded person who likes to do things as opposed to slobbing in front of the telly all day will be of interest.

The activities you've taken part in during your time out can provide useful evidence of the skills you've developed and the qualities you can offer, as will any responsibilities you've undertaken outside family life. Be specific about what you've achieved:

- Fund-raiser for NSPCC: Raised over £9,500 in one year by organising 7 events in the community and through high profile press coverage.

says far more than:

- Member, NSPCC. In charge of fund-raising.

Josephine has shown what she can do (raise £8,000) within a given timescale (a weekend). She has shown she understands the leisure sector and is an active participant in it. She has also included the positions of responsibility she has and outlined her role. Her current voluntary experience with the PTA has helped kept her skills up to date, and enabled her to ask the chair to act as her referee.

Practical skills

Mention anything which could be relevant to the employer, such as:

- Clean driving licence – add any specific class of vehicle you can drive.
- First aid qualifications.
- Public speaking abilities.
- Computer skills.

If these had been more relevant to the role Josephine was applying for, she could have put them higher up her CV. If she was applying for a job as a lifeguard, for example, that would have been appropriate. Work out what fits best for you and the role you want.

Other points of interest

Put your date of birth, marital status and nationality under this section. If you leave off your date of birth, employers will wonder if you're a dinosaur.

Referees

You will need to prepare people to act as referees for you but there is no need to put their details on the CV. Let them know what you're doing, tell them who they might hear from and what you most want them to stress. Don't forget to thank them for their help and let them know how you got on.

Cover any gaps

If you've been off work to raise a family, say so. Keep that section short and include any relevant skills you've got to the post you are applying for. Be positive about what you've done. Remember that employers are seeing more and more people take time out to fulfil personal ambitions or deal with family circumstances. Don't leave gaps; an employer will certainly ask you about them. Make sure all your dates tie up.

The order in which you put information on your CV depends on you. School, college and university leavers normally put their educational qualifications first; they are unlikely to have much work experience. Adults are more likely to put their work experience first. Ultimately, find a format you feel comfortable with. This may mean trying different formats and combinations until you are satisfied.

Examining different styles of CV

There are a number of different styles of CV, most notably the chronological CV (Figure 12) and the functional format (Figure 13).

In both figures 12 and 13, Josephine has used terminology throughout her CV that will appeal to an employer to give him or her as full and accurate a picture as possible of what she can do. Examples included:

Mrs Josephine Ladel
Soupson Cottage
Soup Lane
Littletown
(Home: 0011 111111; Mob: 07800 321 321)
jladel@spoon.com

Career Aspirations
Seeking role within the leisure sector managing a small team of assistants while supporting the management and broadening my managerial and PA experience.

Key Skills and Experience
Serving Committees: organised company quarterly board meetings and those of the PTA. This involved: preparing and sending out agenda, organising location of meetings and refreshments, taking and writing up minutes; following up action points.

Taking responsibility: financial aspects of the family, including budgeting and liaising with utility companies; organised 15 corporate events including Annual Christmas party for 250 at publishing company; liaised with applicants in personnel department.

Checking and maintaining records: verifying qualifications with universities, colleges and employers as stated on applicants' forms and CVs.

Delivering results: my efforts at a publishing company ensured that the provision of secretarial services ran smoothly and applicants for posts within the company were dealt with efficiently. Raised £8,000 for tennis club house through sponsored tennis weekend.

Managing self and others: raised a family while taking on responsibilities outside the house. Met deadlines. Took responsibility for my own learning by enlisting in adult education and open learning programmes.

Work experience
1986–2006	Career break: managed my home and family
1983–1986	Joe Ellen & Co Ltd, Littletown, Publishing company, 100 staff
	Secretary to Managing Director
1981–1983	Joe Ellen & Co Ltd, Littletown
	Secretary to Personnel Manager

Figure 13. A functional CV.

Training, Education and Qualifications

2002–2004	Computer literacy classes: Windows 97, Word Perfect, Powerpoint
	Currently studying Excel through open learning
	Conversational and basic written French acquired at adult education class.
1980–1981	Secretarial College:
	Acquired qualifications in audio typing (40wpm), Shorthand (100wpm) and Secretarial duties
1975–1980	Littletown Girls' School:
	Gained 8 O Levels including Maths, English and French

Hobbies and interests

Parent Teacher Association, Littletown Secondary School Secretary (2002-present); Committee Member and Secretary.

Tennis, Member of local Tennis club committee. Played for the club in the second league.

Badminton; Responsible for refreshment rota weekly during the 2003-4 season. Organised members to serve teas and bake cakes for 40 people. Collected money and paid into bank.

Films, particularly historical in nature.

Additional Skills

Clean driving licence
First aid qualification acquired through St Johns' Ambulance Brigade classes

Points of Interest

Marital status: Married
Nationality: British
Date of Birth: 9 June 1964

References

Available upon request

Figure 13. (continued)

- Responsible for
- Organised corporate events
- Recording up-take on database
- Organised board meetings
- Responsible for smooth running
- Verified with
- Maintained record systems
- Acquired qualifications
- Motivated others

- Liaised with
- Organised
- Raised £8,000
- Played for
- Organised members to
- Collected money
- Currently studying
- Clean driving licence

Use relevant action words such as:

- Highly motivated
- Proven record
- Innovative
- Ability
- Negotiator
- Control
- Career
- Strong work ethic
- Mature
- Loyal
- Committed

- Pragmatic
- Reliable
- Willing and able to learn
- Productive
- Dedicated
- Success/successful
- Achievements
- Promoted
- Enthusiastic
- Capable

Getting feedback

Get at least two people to check your CV for errors and to make suggestions. Careers advisers and Jobcentre Plus personnel will be happy to do this for you. Remember that potential employers will use your CV to go through when you're called for an interview, so do keep a copy to refresh your memory before you go in.

Do it now

- Write up your CV, using lots of action words and measures of your success.
- Work on it until you feel comfortable with it.
- Ask someone to check it for you.
- Then produce another CV for a different role. How far can you tailor the CV to the role and make it relevant?

Summary

It's important to keep your CV relevant and short.

- Re-write your CV for each role – each job and employer is different.

- Include any activities that show you've invested time and energy in developing your skills.

- Remember your CV is your marketing tool. Give it a fresh, crisp look without any errors.

13

Hunting for That Right Role

‛Tell everybody you know what you're looking for. Be specific – don't be vague.’

There are many ways to secure work, both via the Internet and without it, and much depends on how comfortable you are working over your PC to find work, as opposed to making personal contacts.

> You should use a number of methods to find work and not rely on any one alone.

Questions to ask yourself

1. What methods are commonly used to recruit people in this sector?
2. How much time every week are you going to spend looking for work?
3. What is your time-scale for starting work?
4. What barriers and obstacles do you face? What can you do to overcome them?

5. How committed are you to seeing yourself achieve your goal?
6. What are benefits will you gain from returning to work?

It may take a while for you to secure the work you want: those who persist succeed. Remind yourself daily of the benefits you'll gain from returning to work to boost your motivation, commitment and focus.

Think carefully about how and where you are applying

Consider:

- Where are the opportunities for work? Try not to limit your horizons to landing a permanent nine-to-five role. Be more flexible than that, and you're more likely to land the job you want.

- Could you sell your skills and knowledge on a freelance basis to people who need them?

- How does the sector (and employer) you want to work in and for recruit? Word of mouth? Through a particular agency? By advertising in the papers or via the company web site?

- What sorts of methods of recruiting do you feel comfortable with?

Networking for success

Networking is one of the most effective ways to get the job you want, so nurture yours. When employers need to recruit staff, one of the first things they will do if they can't recruit internally is find out whether any of their current personnel know of anyone who might be suitable for the job. They will do this because:

- Those people known to valued employees are a far safer bet than a total unknown. The employee will have a fairly good idea as to how they will fit into the company.

- It is fast.

- It is cheaper than advertising or going through a recruitment company.

So:

> Talk to everybody you know. *Tell* them specifically what you're looking for. Do they know of any companies which would be relevant to you, or people you should approach?

Look through the network of people you know as featured in Figure 6 on page 89 – however long you've known them for – and start getting in touch to find out whether they can give you names and contact details of people they know who work in the sector and for the sort of company you want to be in with. You've then got an introduction to them, although it pays to ask the person who gave you a contact's name to mention they gave you their contact details. You can then write or email with your CV. The advantage of emailing your CV is that it can be quickly passed around a team or section in an organisation whereas paper is more likely to get lost and ignored in a pile.

Connecting with other professionals

This is particularly important if you're looking for a career move when you return to work, as opposed to simply a job. Many professional bodies hold vacancies for employers. Why not visit the web site of the organisation which is relevant to you and see if yours does? Meantime, raise your profile and get seen, maybe at local events or areas where people working in the sector are known to socialise and meet. Aim to build up relationships with them and get involved in projects which are going on locally. It's a great way to show people what you can do once you put your mind, skills and capabilities to it. Remember that networking is a two way process – find out if there is anything you can do for those who are helping you. If there isn't, ask them to keep you in mind for a later date.

Ask for names to write to, not just in Human Resources (HR), but the person in charge of the area you want to get into. Send both HR and that person your CV and follow it up with a phone call. Even if your contact does not think they are recruiting, there's nothing to stop you sending in your CV, because HR and line-managers may have a far clearer idea of what their current and future recruitment needs are than your contact.

If you're doing a college course, find out what networks your course tutors and the college careers service has with local employers – they may know of someone who is recruiting. A stint of work experience often leads to job offers. Keep in touch without being pushy or demanding. Always write a thank-you note for any help you've been given.

Unsolicited applications

If you want to work for one particular place, you could always contact them with your CV by mail or email to see if they are interested in you and your skills. The problem with this approach is that you don't know whether they actually need to take anyone on. Try to target your sales pitch at a time when you have clues that they might need extra staff, such as towards the Christmas period when stores are going to be busy if you want to work in retail, or if you've read in the news that they are expanding or opening a bigger branch which will lead to opportunities. If someone has given you the name of the company and the person you're calling, mention them.

Example

Eleanor Rushton wants to work in retail, specifically with books. She gets through to her local bookshop and to the manager there.

Eleanor: *Good morning. My name is Eleanor Rushton and I'm calling to ask about any vacancies you may have for a sales assistant.*

Mr Smith: *I'm sorry, I'm not taking on any staff at the moment.*

Eleanor: *Are you likely to be taking on anyone in the future, perhaps just before Christmas?*

Mr Smith: *Yes, I usually take a couple of part-time staff on then.*

Eleanor: *Could I send you my CV to look at? I've got experience of helping in a clothes shop, but really I want to work with books. I've just completed my English Literature A level and I read very widely, and I enjoy working with people. I've been into your shop several times and would love to work there.*

Mr Smith: *Well, that sounds of interest. Can you drop your CV in to me and we can have a chat? Would you be looking for full-time or part-time work?*

Eleanor: *I'm happy to start with part-time work, at the moment. I'd be flexible. I'll drop my CV in this afternoon.*

Mr Smith: *That's fine. I'll be here, then, and so we can have a brief chat about it.*

Eleanor now has to get ready to take her CV, already prepared, to Mr Smith. She dresses carefully, notes her reasons for wanting to work with books and people, and reminds herself of the experience she's got which would be useful to Mr Smith. In addition, as Christmas is approaching, she notes that her experience as a parent will benefit her as people ask for advice in choosing books for children. Here she is showing how her career break experience and skills can benefit a potential employer. They are, in this case, relevant. She needs to think of all the things she can bring to the bookshop which someone else can't. So you see, you can turn a phone call to your advantage without being pushy.

Companies' premises

Companies and small businesses often put up signs if they are recruiting, or you can simply walk into a store and ask.

Don't forget the power of the information meeting.

There's nothing to stop you getting in touch with a contact whose name you've been given and asking them if you can meet briefly. Explain where you are and that you'd like their advice in terms of how you should approach your job hunt, or what strategies you might use to boost your chances of success. Talk to them a bit about your career aspirations and what you have to offer and you may well hook their interest sufficiently that they want to meet you. There's nothing worse than the possibility of losing someone who is enthusiastic and keen to a competitor!

Why not email your CV?

Employers like taking on people who find them through the web. It shows an interest in their organisation and that the job hunter is adept at using IT.

Going through the Internet

There are many Internet sites advertising vacancies on-line, such as *www.reed.co.uk* and *www.monster.co.uk*. They have lots of practical advice and tips on how to write a CV, interview technique, salary assessment tools, so that you can see if you're being paid at the right rate, career resources, assessment exercises. Most advertise their vacancies on their site, you click on those which interest you for more information and to apply. You can register for email alerts of new vacancies as they come in and many sites give you the facility to post your CV for employers with recruitment needs to consider.

Visit employers' web sites

As we saw in Chapter 7, many organisations advertise vacancies on their web sites – it's cheap, fast and it hooks people who are naturally interested in them. To find companies in the sector you wish to work in, run a search through an engine such as Google or Yahoo. Have a good look at the sites you find. In particular, look at the locations they are situated in. Their head office may be in a city like London, but they may have many satellite locations all over the UK, so do your homework thoroughly. Check the recruitment page to find out if they are recruiting. Even if they aren't, you could still email your CV, appropriately tailored, to various people within the organisation to ask about opportunities.

Advantages of using the Internet

- It has a global reach – your search isn't limited to local opportunities.

- It can be particularly useful if your partner's firm is relocating you – you could arrive with a new job all set up!

- You can job hunt from home.

- It doesn't cost anything.

- Even the smallest company can benefit from it.

- Most sites are regularly updated.

- Most sites have lots of invaluable links so follow them up; you never know where they will lead.

- You can use the Internet and pc to check job vacancies on-line, do research, email your CV, set up your own business's web site, market your own CV, email companies and agencies...

The disadvantages

- Go with well known sites for security purposes, especially if you're going to give personal details over the Net

- It lacks the personal touch.

Using recruitment agencies

Agencies are of two kinds:

1. Specialist; they focus on a specific sector, such as nursing, education, engineering, secretarial, hotel and catering, accountancy, the media, legal work, and the like.
2. Generalist with different sections focusing in on specific sectors or areas of work.

The agencies in your area will be listed in *Yellow Pages* or you can also check them out on-line.

Choosing your agency

Try to find out which ones have the best reputation in your area by talking to people who have used them. Walk in and pay them a visit – do you get a warm welcome? Does the place look professional and are there quiet confidential meeting rooms where you can talk to a consultant?

Find out what an agency's track record is like before you sign up for it. The longer it has existed, the more likely it is to have a strong network of employers who use its services, which means more choice for you. Choose an agency which specialises in your niche area where the consultants will have a thorough understanding of the career paths available in it. That said, some agencies are sufficiently large that you have specialist divisions with staff who have built up an expertise of it over the years. It is important that you feel comfortable with the agency you're working with. After all, they are representing you.

Find out what extras your agency offers. Does it offer free training, for example, and networking events for its customers? Check out the web site: does it show links to the professional organisations in the sectors it works in, and does it have advice on its pages for job hunters? Many agencies have news items, with results from surveys, which make interesting reading and could give you new ideas in terms of finding work or approaching your job hunt or even career path.

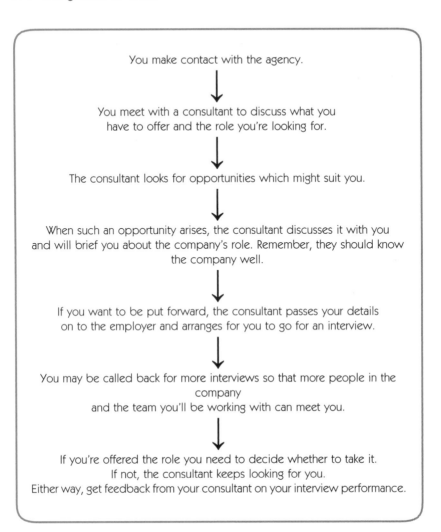

Figure 14. The job hunting process through a recruitment agency

Handling that first meeting

When you go into an agency, dress as if you were going for an interview. You'll be asked to complete a form with details about your contact points, background, qualifications and skills. You'll meet a consultant, who'll find out more about where you are in your career and what you want to do next; what your career aspirations are and what you feel you can contribute. Your consultant should spend time getting to know you before putting you up for any vacancies; if they don't spend time finding out about you, you wonder how much they know about the employers they're helping in the recruitment process.

At the end of your meeting, find out by what means and how often your consultant prefers to keep in touch. Check your mobile and email regularly; recruitment can move fast, and you don't want to miss out on opportunities because your mobile was switched off, or you did not check your emails.

Do:
- Use other methods to find work as well as an agency.
- Be flexible.
- Ask for feedback after you've been to interviews and expect to be briefed before you go.
- Treat your consultant as a human being; a thank-you goes a long way.

Don't:
- Pay the agency anything – the employer who recruits you does that.
- Be pushed into the first job you get offered
- Turn down a temporary post while waiting for a permanent one – you never know where it could lead.

Consider temp to perm

You may be offered the chance to start with an organisation as a temp. If the role sounds as though it might suit, even for a short time, consider it. Once you've been given a chance and proved yourself, the company may well try to hang on to you. Temps are tried and tested; they know how the organisation works and it's a chance for them and the employer to see how well they all get on together.

Responding to advertisements

There are various places you can look for job advertisements.

a) newspapers and magazines
b) Internet sites
c) professional bodies
d) companies' premises.

Newspapers and magazines

There are a number of opportunities here. Most newspapers, both local and regional press, and the nationals, have job pages, some on specific days, and web sites on which vacancies are also listed. Recruitment pages may appear in the printed press on specific days of the week, such as a Thursday; or the larger papers may carry vacancies related to specific sectors on certain days of the week, for example in the *Guardian*, the profile is:

Monday	Media
Tuesday	Education
Wednesday	Public sector
Thursday	Engineering, computing
Saturday	Media

Many papers have a jobs section, not only with a whole host of vacancies, but also advice and tips for job hunters about the recruitment process. They will also list any job fairs coming up in your area – a great way to talk to people about what opportunities they have. There are also a number of freebies, given away at railway stations and tube stops, or retail outlets in your area, which all host job vacancy pages.

Before applying – do your research

If you see an advert in the paper, it's important to do as much research as you can before you send in your application. Sometimes this is difficult to do, because the name of the company isn't on the advert, or the application is minimal. Look at the clues you're given.

Professional and trade magazines often have vacancies in the back so they are worth getting.

Reading job advertisements

The following examples are included to show you the sort of clues you can look for.

Mr Willing is General Manager of Let's Go Holidays. He wants to recruit several staff, so he places several advertisements in the local paper. If you look closely, you'll see that there are several preferences in the three advertisements below and some absolutely necessities in each case.

WANTED

Person to help out in the office

9:00 – 5:00 Monday – Friday

Must be cheerful, presentable and willing to do anything!

Apply in writing: Mr Willing, Let's Go Holidays,

31 High Street, Middletown XX1 5DJ

Mr Willing wants someone who will turn up, be cheerful and willing to muck in with anything required – someone who won't turn their nose up at doing the more basic routine tasks. You need to show him you're the sort of person who will happily do anything that is thrown at you – you're a team-spirited person.

Mr Willing has also had to recruit sales staff, because his head office want to expand the presence of Let's Go Holidays in his town. So he places another advert.

> **WANTED**
> **Full-Time Sales Staff**
> Must have good communication skills, be able to work
> under pressure and to meet targets.
> High drive and IT skills essential.
> Experience in the travel industry an advantage.
> Apply in writing: Mr Willing, Let's Go Holidays,
> 31 High Street, Middletown XX1 5DJ

This advertisement demands people with specific skills, i.e. those who can:

- Communicate effectively.

- Work fast under pressure without losing their cool.

- Meet targets set by head office and relayed to Mr Willing, whose job it is to make sure that his sales staff all know what their targets are and can meet them.

- Show they have a high drive, which refers to their motivation to succeed and their hunger to achieve.

- Use information technology – Mr Willing doesn't want to have to teach people IT from scratch.

He would *prefer* to recruit sales personnel who have worked in the travel industry before, but he is not excluding anyone who hasn't.

Mr Willing has also decided to take on a part-time Training Officer to ensure his staff are getting the training they need to meet their targets. He places one more advertisement.

> **WANTED**
> **Part-Time Experienced Training Officer**
> **20 hours a week**
> Enthusiastic, motivating approach essential.
> Experience of training in travel industry essential.
> Apply in writing: Mr Willing, Let's Go Holidays,
> 31 High Street, Middletown XX1 5DJ

Mr Willing is asking for communication skills (trainers need to be able to work with a wide variety of people) but he is also expecting a trainer who can think about meeting the needs of an expanding business and produce tailor-made courses to help his people meet their targets. He *definitely* wants someone who has worked in the travel industry and would exclude anyone who didn't have it (unless they could win him over!).

> If you see an advert which appeals, analyse it. What could the position contribute to the organisation and its goals?

Creating new strategies

If you can, why not offer your services to companies who need cover while their staff are on holiday. Once you've got your foot in the door and proved your worth, they're less likely to let you go!

Get some work experience

This is especially the case if you're changing career and moving on to something new. Even if you're going to be in a company for one day a week for a few weeks, you can build up a huge amount of experience and knowledge, and update your skills, while proving your commitment and interest in your new career. Work experience gives you a strategic advantage: you're in the right place at the right time if the company wants to take someone on with your skills. It gives people the chance to test you and see if you fit in with their culture and image. If they find someone who meets all the criteria they're looking for, who is personally known to them, they are more likely to recruit via this sort of networking and experience route. There may be short- or long-term projects you can do for them which will lead to other things. People who are tried and tested are less of a risk to recruit.

Ask them for their advice and any names they can give you to show you're not putting all your eggs in one basket:

- Do you know of anyone who is recruiting at the moment who would be interested in my CV?

- What would you be doing if you were in my position?

- This is what I've done so far to find work in this sector. Is there anything else I should be doing?

Other strategies you could employ include:

1. Working for one or two days a week while you're looking to land a full time job.
2. Learning from others' success stories. Ask people you know in work how they got in.
3. Starting out in temporary positions until the right permanent one comes up – why not find out if there is a project you can do for a company, or work for them short term?
4. Being persistent – it can take time to find the right role. Give up, and you fail. Persist and you'll succeed.

Invest the time in your job search

Sending a couple of applications in every week and looking idly through the evening paper won't get you very far unless you really are lucky. Spend 30 to 40 hours a week on your job search, if you're looking for a full-time role, and 15–20 if you want something part time.

Every week check to see that you have:

Attended any careers fairs in your area to talk to people about returning to work ☐

Followed up any new leads or contacts people have given you ☐

Researched more companies to follow up ☐

Been in touch with your recruitment consultant at any agencies you've signed up with ☐

Looked at company web sites and their recruitment pages for details of any new roles or developments ☐

Looked at your local Learning and Skills council's web sites for details of any new initiatives to get people back into work ☐

Checked Internet job sites for new vacancies ☐

Looked at your email for any email alerts of new relevant vacancies which have come in ☐

Talked to at least 10 people in your network to see if they can suggest people for you to talk to ☐

Attended any professional groups or support networks in your area who've held meetings ☐

Looked in the local press recruitment pages or national papers ☐

Gone to ask for any specialist help you need ☐

Got your CV or applications checked before you sent them out ☐

Kept track of all the CVs and applications you've sent out ☐

Continued to develop your skills ☐

You may want to rely more heavily on some methods to find work than others.

> **Persistence pays off!**

> **Do it now**

- Find out how your sector recruits staff. Is there a difference between the way in which small, medium and large organisations recruit?
- Prepare a 30-second talk which specifically outlines what you want to do at work and what you can offer.
- Identify three events you can attend locally where you won't know people. Attend, and aim to tell at least 5 people about your career goals. Use your 30-second talk.
- Remind yourself of the benefits you'll gain by returning to work.

Summary

There are many ways to secure work and it's important to build your confidence in handling them.

- Make good use of any events run locally which give you advice on the recruitment process.

- Network, network, network.

- If you are a parent, do not talk about your children when meeting people. They are not interested in them. Talk about what you can offer and contribute yourself.

14

Writing to Apply

6Time spent on an application is more likely to lead to success.9

When you're approaching an employer, you want to attract their interest in you by demonstrating that you:

1. Have the skills and capabilities they need.
2. Have done some research into them sufficiently to believe that the two of you should talk more – you think you'll be a good fit.
3. Have tremendous enthusiasm for what you want to do.

Evaluating the job

If you're responding to an advertised post, get as much information as you can before you send an application in. You can do this by emailing, telephoning or writing. Find out if there is an information pack and a job description, or whether you need to complete an application form. Check the organisation's web site for any further clues to the job. If the company has advertised the post for the world to see, it probably means that they don't have anyone who can fill the post internally, unless they want to compare applicants unknown to them against their own candidates.

When the information arrives, read through it and work out whether you want to go for it and apply or not. Much of this will depend on your reaction to what you're reading and hearing about the role and the organisation. When you're looking at the job description:

> Focus on the things you can do and work out strategies for handling those you cannot.

Women tend to focus too much on the things they cannot do, while men are the opposite. Each job will have a set of criteria an employer definitely needs, as we saw with Mr Willing of Let's Go Holidays. On the information you have about the post, tick those things you can do. Look at those you cannot. Could you do them if you had training, or get training while you were applying? Would they be 'nice-to-have' items in a potential candidate from an employer's point of view?

Have you worked out:

- What skills the employer wants? ☐
- Specific qualifications they need? ☐
- Qualities they are asking for? ☐
- Any additional points? ☐
- What values they hold, e.g. target driven, caring, family friendly? ☐
- What message they are giving about career progression opportunities and the role itself? ☐

The more research you do the better prepared you will be to go through the entire selection process. Employers can see when an applicant for a specific post or someone writing on spec has done their research and thought about their application. If you can, visit the company – their showrooms, perhaps or a branch, and ask for information about their products and services. And an absolute *must* is to check out their web site.

Reminding yourself of your assets

Before you start writing to an employer, remind yourself what you've got to offer and why the company you're contacting appeals.

Have you:

Identified the skills you have which they require and prefer? (Remember, you don't have to acquired them through paid employment.) ☐

Noted any qualities you've got which would be particularly relevant to the position? ☐

Researched the company thoroughly so that you know what its values and ethos are, what it's all about? ☐

Checked you've got the qualifications required or preferred, if any? ☐

Thought about what the employer will be wanting and what the role will contribute to the organisation? ☐

Got your CV ready to adapt to this particular employer and role? ☐

Prepared your unique selling points? ☐

Developed strategies for those areas you cannot cover or aren't sure about? ☐

Some golden rules

If an employer is advertising a post, you may simply be asked to send in a CV by mail or email (more usual for local and family firms). Whether the ad asks for it or not, send a covering letter or email attaching your CV and explaining what you think you can bring to the post and the company and what appeals about them, but be brief. Your covering letter shouldn't be any more than a page of A4. Lay your letter out properly and make sure there are no grammatical or spelling errors.

Increase your chances from the start

Do whatever the employer asks you to do. If they want an application form completed and sent back, do that. If they want your CV, send it. They may have specific reasons for the manner in which they ask you to send in your details. Failure to follow their request may well result in rejection.

Take care over your application

There are some simple do's and don't's to follow to boost your chances of success, whether you're applying or a specific role or writing on spec:

Do	Don't
Check your spelling	Send in spelling errors
Use a clean white piece of paper	Use flowery notepaper, paper covered with coffee stains and creases
Check your grammar	Send in errors – if you can't be bothered to check your work in an application, why should you bother when you're at work?

Do	Don't
Word process it	Handwrite it (unless specifically asked to do so)
Keep a copy of everything you send out – you'll need to refresh your memory before your interview	Lose track of what applications are going out where. Keep them in a file and make a top cover note of who has been sent what and when
Be honest	Try to cover up any gaps – employers will immediately wonder what you've been doing
Check the spelling and title of the person you're writing to	Start letters with Dear Sir/Madam if you can avoid it – try to find out the name of the person who is handling the recruitment process
Make the whole thing easy to read and relevant	Include any information about your kids, grandchildren or anything which isn't relevant to the post you're applying for
Send in any documents you've been asked to include	Send in copies of all your certificates etc. unless you've been asked to do so

Finally, don't be witty or clever, or sound guilty about taking time out. Do you know of someone who *hasn't* taken time out? Employers aren't interested in any guilt you have. They want to know what you can do for them.

Completing application forms

Before you do anything else, copy the form itself and practise completing it before you start the final copy you'll send in. It gives you an opportunity to see how your answers will fit into the space available. Also copy the final result, before you put it into the post, so that you can refer to it before you go for an interview.

You may be sorely tempted when faced with an application form to put 'see attached CV' in neat writing instead of answering all the questions on the form itself but don't. Make the required effort and complete the form. Employers use application forms as a way to compare applicants for the position they wish to fill, so don't throw your chances away. Answer the questions carefully and consider the possible reasons an employer has included each one. For example, how does each question relate to the job you're applying for? What will it give you the opportunity to tell the person reading the form about yourself and how you might fit in with the organisation?

> Every single question is there for a reason.

Don't leave any questions unanswered. Many larger employers scan application forms now and any gaps will result in your form going into the bin. Many of the questions may ask you about your transferable skills, such as the way you'd handle situations and people, problems you've had to overcome at work, achievements you're particularly proud of, or what you've contributed to an organisation before. Don't forget that you can use any voluntary work you've done to give examples here, as much as paid work situations. Use scenarios you've been in that are relevant to the post you want to have, i.e. that which you are applying for.

You don't necessarily need to word process the form – look for instructions on how to proceed and follow them. If you're writing with a pen, use black ink; it shows up better than blue when photocopied by you and the employer.

Making the most of the further information section

This section provides you with a great chance to blow your trumpet. The company is, in effect, saying 'Tell us about yourself' or 'Is there anything else we should know about you which would be of interest to us?' They ask you to write a short couple of paragraphs about why you want the position on offer, or why you want to work for that company. They may want to see what your written skills are like, how persuasive you are in writing, how much research you've done into the company and job involved. Whatever form it takes, use the chance to sell yourself – don't leave it blank! You could consider outlining:

- Your career aspirations.
- The skills you have and the qualities you offer.
- What has motivated you to return to work; (don't mention money or hours here).
- The sort of role and career you're looking for and what you can contribute;
- Any achievements you're particularly proud of, and the skills and qualities you need to make them happen.
- What appeals to you about the role and the company – a great chance to mention any research you've done about them.

Practise this section several times. Don't complete it for real until you're absolutely happy with the practice version.

Composing a covering letter

This is an important marketing tool which introduces you and sets the scene for your CV, whether you send it by email or post. If you email your CV, your email should include two or three paragraphs explaining,

- Why you are writing and how you heard of the vacancy if you're responding to an advert.
- Why you are applying and mentioning (briefly) relevant experience and what you can offer.
- Why the company appeals.
- When you could meet for an interview.

If you're sending a letter with your CV, as you certainly should do if you're applying by post, type your introductory letter, unless you're asked to handwrite it – some companies analyse your writing to see what your personality is like and how you will fit into their culture.

Always include any job reference advertised with the post – this will help to create the right image at the company's end. It shows you pay attention to detail.

Make sure you sound really keen and enthusiastic about the role and the organisation – and don't make the mistake of starting off *I'm looking for a part-time job to fit in with my children.* While that may be the case, it won't impress.

Follow your application up with a phone call

Once you've responded to the advert and sent your CV and covering letter in, follow up with a phone call to make sure it's arrived safely. You could take the opportunity to talk to both HR and the person in charge of the area you're applying to work in. Similarly, if you're applying on spec, there's nothing to stop you following up any contact you make to make sure your details arrived safely and to see if there's any other information the employer needs.

Do it now

- Draft a covering letter.
- Work out what you would put to the request 'Please provide us with any additional information that would help us in the selection process.'
- Visualise yourself in your new job. What does it feel like?

Summary

Always sell yourself to an employer by showing him or her how the company will benefit from taking you on and what you can contribute to the role you want.

- Don't forget to explain why the employer appeals to you – massage their egos a bit!

- If you can refer to research you've done, do so – it shows you're serious.

	(Put your address here)
	(The date)
Call the company to get the right name and title of the person to write to.	Mrs Holmes Title (Company name and address)
	Dear Mrs Holmes
Give the job reference if there was one.	<u>Job Vacancy RG7</u>
Explain why you are writing and how you heard of the vacancy.	I am writing to apply for the above vacancy for a Customer Services Agent which was advertised in the *Evening Echo* on Friday 18 November.
Explain why you are applying and mention (briefly) relevant experience and what you can offer.	I am looking for a post in a customer service environment in the health care sector. You will see from my CV that I have three years' front-line experience in a charity shop, and I enjoy working with a wide variety of people. I particularly enjoy helping people.
Explain why the company appeals.	<u>Your organisation appeals because I would love to work in the health care private sector.</u> I have visited several hospitals in our area and have been really impressed with the staff I have met so far in your organisation.
Explain when you could meet for interview.	I enclose my CV for your information and would be delighted to attend for an interview at any time. I can be contacted at my home number on 0111 11111.
Finish politely.	I look forward to hearing from you.
If you start Dear Sir/Madam, put Yours faithfully instead of yours sincerely.	Yours sincerely
	(sign your name here)
	Sarah Spot

Figure 15. Writing a letter enclosing a CV.

15

Interviewing...You and Them

Don't forget: interviews are a two way process.

Interviews are often nerve-racking experiences, but the thing to keep uppermost in your mind is that they are a two way process – you're interviewing the employer as much as the other way around. Thorough practical and mental preparation will boost your chances of success. In fact, if you've done your homework properly and sent off a number of CVs, you should have several interviews lined up.

There are some excellent books written on the subject of interviews, and you would be well advised to invest some time in heading out to your local library and having a good read. You'll find the titles listed under Further Reading. In the meantime, here are some tips and practical advice!

Right interview, wrong day

When you get called in for an interview, congratulate yourself! You've made a sufficiently favourable impression that the employer wants to meet you and learn more about you to find out whether you'll fit in the team you'll be working with and the company itself.

> Practical preparations will go a long way to helping you focus on what's important and boost your chances of success.

Find out where you're going and how you're going to get there

In preparation for your interview, have you:

- Found out how to get there? ☐
- Made sure you're going to the right place? (Some organisations are based on several sites.) ☐
- Worked out how you're going to get there? ☐
- Allowed for possible problems en route? ☐
- Taken the time of day into account? For example, will there be problems with traffic if you need to travel in rush hour? ☐
- Worked out where you're going to park, if you're driving? ☐
- Put the date in your diary and allowed plenty of time before and after it? ☐
- Made sure your car has plenty of petrol? ☐
- Got change for parking in case you need it? ☐

Dressing the part

Wear something which is appropriate for the sector you're going to work in. If you've done your research, you'll know whether it's safe to go for a casual–smart look or a business suit. Tone down the make-up, jewellery and perfume or after-shave – you're going for an interview, not a date. If in doubt, dress smartly rather than casually.

Attention to detail matters

It sounds obvious and you've probably been telling your children to do this for years but a few days *before* the day of your interview, check:

- Is your interview outfit clean? ☐
- Is it neatly pressed? ☐
- Does your hair need cutting? ☐
- Are your shoes clean and well heeled? ☐
- Have you allowed time to shower and wash your hair and nails on the day? ☐
- Have you got an outfit ready for a second interview, if required? ☐
- Checked the company web site and done an Internet search for any news items on it? ☐
- Re-read your CV and application? ☐
- Thought about questions you want to ask the interviewers? ☐
- Thought about what you need to know at this stage? ☐
- Considered your worth in the market? ☐
  (You should get salary comparisons for this by talking to recruitment consultants, doing salary assessments on Internet web sites such as *www.reed.co.uk*, weighing up your financial needs and what difference perks will make to any salary offer.)
- Considered questions they will want to ask you? ☐
- Worked out how you're going to cover any gaps in your CV. ☐
- Worked out how you're going to deal with any weaknesses you have in your application? ☐

Understanding the process

Employers are assessing prospective recruits through several methods to give them a better idea of whether you're the right person for the vacancy they want to fill. These could include:

- Testing the specific skills you need for the position you're applying for – for example, you might be asked to teach a class for an hour, if you're applying for a job as a teacher.

- A literacy, numeracy or non-verbal reasoning test.

- A work-place simulating test, seeing how you perform – how well do you work under pressure, how hungry you are to succeed, accuracy, or to enable the employer to assess particular skills he wants.

- A personality test to determine your strengths and weaknesses.

- Hand-writing tests to assess your character.

- Group exercises to see how well you work in a team and what sort of role you naturally veer towards.

- Presentation skills to see how you can influence people, present information and think on your feet.

- Psychometric tests.

You should be told what will be expected of you, and whether or not you will need to prepare anything in advance. There are more books on the market which go into greater detail (see Further Reading) and you can also get advice from careers personnel at agencies and job centres. Interviews are, however, the most popular way to start assessing candidates, and you may be called back two or three times to meet different people. Welcome this opportunity. In these days when it's essential to get the right mix in the team, personality is everything, and that is hard to assess in one interview alone. The more you get a chance to find out what your potential colleagues are like, the better.

Preparing questions and answers

It's difficult to work out what you'll be asked in advance, although there are some tried and tested questions interviewers favour. These days, employers are more likely to ask you questions to help them ascertain what sort of personality you have, and how you will work in the team dynamics that exist in the company or the section you're going to join. They will want you to demonstrate how you've used transferable skills and may give you a test to see how competent you are in the job-specific ones you'll need on the job. In short, they want to find out more about you and expand their knowledge of what you can do, often based on what you have written in your CV or application form.

Your CV will give them a good idea of your skills base and experience; they now want to expand on your CV and discover whether you both have a long future together i.e. whether they can meet your career aspirations. Recruiting is a costly business and there's no point in taking someone on if they leave six months later because the organisation is at odds with their career plans.

That said, if they are interviewing several candidates, employers may have a prescribed set of questions to ask everyone so that they can compare the answers. Some questions will be more heavily weighted than others in terms of ranking, so that if there is a specific area they need to really question candidates on, there will be more questions on this subject than others. Nonetheless, you should have the opportunity to ask plenty of questions yourself to make sure you're getting the answers you need to make the right decision for you.

'So tell us about yourself!'

This is a favourite first question from interviewers, but it is amazing how many people don't prepare for it. The interviewers are not looking for a reply like this:

> Well, I'm 38 years old, and I've got brown hair and I'm five feet four. I've got three children, Samuel aged 10, Judith who is 8 and Michael who's, umm, 6. Now that they're all at school – St

> *Joseph's in Layton, it's really good and they love it – I thought it was time I went back to work.*

The interviewers are not interested in your children. They are interested in you, and what you can do for them, your career aspirations, skills and competences. They want to know what sort of person you are, and whether you'll fit in well with the company and your potential colleagues. So something this would be far more appropriate:

> *I've spent 10 years raising children. Now that they are older, I've decided it's time to go back to work. A career as a financial adviser seems to meet all the criteria I'm looking for and I think I could contribute a lot – I've taken a course in IT to update my skills and I can communicate clearly with people and enjoy helping them. I read the financial pages in the paper regularly and have made all the financial decisions about our home and money over the last 10 years. I will relate well to people who've got a family and are looking to provide security for them in the coming years. I'm really looking forward to my move back to work.*

This second answer shows the interviewer that the candidate has:

- updated her IT skills, recognising that she will need them in the workplace;
- skills and a passion for helping and advising people;
- experience that will benefit the company;
- the ability to relate to the company's customers and situations they are facing;
- the willingness to learn;
- an interest in the subject – she reads the financial pages of the papers regularly.

The answer has given the interviewers plenty more to ask her about.

Anticipating questions

It's very important to prepare this because some companies may conduct an interview with you over the phone to decide whether to take your application on further, or to offer you a job on the spot. Questions you may be asked include:

- What are your strengths and weaknesses?
- Why do you want to work for us? Why not our competitors?
- Why should we recruit you over someone else?
- What do you know about our company?
- Where do you see yourself being in five years' time?
- Why are you coming back to work?
- What's most important to you in your next career move?
- What interests you about this role? What could you contribute to it?
- What will your referees tell us about you?

There may be also be a number of questions designed to find out how you handle different situations to give the interviewers insight into your personality.

- Tell us about a problem you've had to solve. How did you approach it and what was the outcome?

- Give us an example of something you've done that you're particularly proud of.

- Tell us about a difficult situation you had to deal with. How did you handle it and what was the outcome? What would you do differently next time?

If you don't understand a question, ask the interviewer to repeat it; and if you need more time to consider your answer, say so. Don't waffle on – keep your answers short, punchy and relevant. Employers are not supposed to ask you about your arrangements for looking after dependants – some will assume that since you're applying for work, you'll have taken care of this anyway. Don't say you're returning for the money even if it's true or that you like the sound of the post because the hours appeal. Talk about what interests you in it.

So what should you ask them?

This is your big chance to find out more about the organisation and people you could be working with, so make the most of it! Think about what you want to find out in order to decide whether the employer is right for you, and will be able to provide you with the opportunities you want to achieve your career goals.

- Tell me about the management structure here.

- What training is available to me?

- Where is the job situated?

- How is the team I'll be working with structured? How many people are in it and how long have they been with the organisation?

- How does this organisation assess staff performance?

- Am I replacing someone or is this a new post?

- What happened to the previous post-holder?

- Tell me how you joined the company (to interviewer). What do you like about it?

- Where does the company see itself being in the next five years?

- Who will I be reporting to?

- What is the next step (i.e. where do we go from here)?

Handling interviewers

You should aim to arrive at least 15 minutes before your interview to give yourself time to freshen up and take a look around the reception area where you wait. Ask if you can use the ladies' or men's – it will give you a first chance to assess how the company treats visitors and staff alike. Are there fresh towels and soap for example? If you are offered a coffee while you're waiting, is it delivered to you promptly in a mug, a cup and saucer or a plastic cup? Do the people there look happy to be working there and is the atmosphere a buzzy one? Could you see yourself walking into the office every week looking forward to working there?

What will happen in the interview?

If there is more than one interviewer, make sure you make eye contact with everyone as you answer a question, although you can focus on the questioner. Smile, however nervous you're feeling.

Listen well

If you're listening to something that's being said, nod to show you're listening, make agreeing noises, such as *'yes, I see,'* at regular intervals. Don't interrupt the interviewer in the middle of a sentence, however often he or she may do the same to you.

Keep your hand gestures to a minimum. Don't fidget or put your hands in your pockets. Rest them comfortably on your lap. Avoid slouching, sit upright, leaning forward slightly.

Don't get chummy

Apart from the first few moments when the interviewer may be seeking to put you at your ease, try not to talk about your children, pets, the difficulty of parking in the area or what you did last Friday night, however friendly he or she appears to be. Keep to the point – the job, the company, and what you can contribute, plus your career goals.

Show you've done your research

At any opportunity you can, show you've done some research. Even if you've just walked into the sales area and had a good look around, that shows you've taken an interest and done *something*. If you've noticed an article on the company in the paper which was positive or talked about new products and services, say so. Comment on the organisation's web site to show you've visited it.

Don't leave them wondering why they should recruit you.

Listen to this familiar comment made by the manager of a supermarket chain after an interview with an applicant, Janice:

Case Study: Janice, attending an interview

'She talked a lot about what our company could do for her, putting lots of emphasis on our training programmes and career progression routes. She made the right noises there. But I'm still left wondering, *What can she do for us?'*

Finally, some practical tips

Don't:

- smoke or drink even if the interviewer(s) do;
- lie – you're bound to get found out;
- ask about pay early on – wait until the interviewer introduces it.

Following up

Take a deep breath! It's over! When you have left the building and got away, take a deep breath and congratulate yourself. You've done it! You got through it. Reflect on what you handled well and which questions you found difficult. How did you handle the difficult interviewers and how would you do things differently next time? If you went through a recruitment agency to apply for the post, give your consultant a call later on to find out whether she had any feedback and to let her know what you thought.

What happens next?

You may be asked back for a second and even a third interview, perhaps to meet more of the team you'll be working with, or even to do a presentation or take part in games to show how well you work in a team.

You may have been offered the job on the spot. Don't accept it at once. Tell the interviewers you've enjoyed meeting them and that you'll get back to them. They would want to do the same in your shoes. Ask them to put any offer they make to you in writing. Talk salary, terms and conditions.

You could also be asked to consider another role. It could be that your skills and personality are better suited to another part of the organisation, and the company doesn't want to lose you. Ask for another meeting and go away to find out more. This is your career we're talking about, and you'll be working in it for around 45 weeks or more of the year, so it's important you make every effort to reassure yourself it's the right move for you.

Learn from 'No thanks, not this time'

You may receive a letter rejecting you and yes, you may feel disappointed, unless you realised the role and company was not right for you. Ask for feedback on your performance and how you might improve it next time. Think carefully back to the whole process. Ask yourself questions such as:

1. Should you have been better prepared?
2. Were you suitably attired for the interview?
3. Did you handle the questions well?
4. Were you picking up signals that things weren't quite right?
5. Did your heart tell you something was missing?

Often we know when something isn't just 100% right for us, and sometimes, although we are disappointed to get the 'No thanks' call or letter, we can have that gut reaction, 'No, it wasn't right for me.'

It's worth remembering, however, that it simply could be that the successful candidate was a better fit into the team. Much goes on personality these days; another candidate could have been a closer fit with the team than you were. Somewhere, another team will be exactly right for you and you'll be exactly right for it.

Reflect and move on

You can spend hours and days dwelling on your *'No thanks'* response, or you can get into your next gear and start looking at what you're going to do next. Moping won't move you closer to your goal. Reflecting, assessing, learning from the experience and moving swiftly on, will.

Do it now

- Give a friend the list of questions you might be asked in an interview. Get them to give you a mock interview. Why not practise on each other?
- 'Tell us about yourself.' What would you say?
- What gives you an advantage over other applicants?

Summary

Preparation is the key to success in any interview and will help take a lot of your nerves away.

- Be prepared to go back for two or three interviews.

- Relax – don't get too tense!

- Take in as much of the environment as you can when you attend for an interview so that you can assess whether you would be happy working there.

- After you have left the interview, reflect on the way you handled yourself. What can you learn from the process that will help you do even better next time?

16

Blasting Barriers

‘Always bear in mind that your own resolution to succeed is more important than any one thing.’

Abraham Lincoln

As you move along your journey to return to work, you may hit any number of barriers and obstacles which come up in your path. This chapter will help you overcome many of them. Be creative in finding solutions and make the most of the help and support out there – not just friends and family – to help you handle any problem areas.

Resistance from friends and family

You'll have some people in your life who've got used to you not working. It suits them. They can call on you in emergencies and in fact, it's going to upset their apple cart if you go back to work. As a result, they may try to put you off and sabotage your attempts to return to work, perhaps by:

1. making off-hand comments about your prospects relating to your age or the length of time you've been out of work;

2. making sweeping statements about the opportunities ahead of you, what employers are looking for – they sound as though they are experts and put doubt in your mind;
3. giving you examples of how people have tried and failed;
4. making barriers you've got to overcome appear bigger than they truly are.

The key is to develop strategies to handle them, such as questioning and challenging their beliefs and statements.

Elderly relatives

The problem with elderly relatives is that no one knows how much longer they are going to live for. There are no given time scales as there are with children. By the time your children are in their late teens, they should be fairly independent and, if they are living at home, playing their part in the running and upkeep of the house. But young children and elderly relatives can be equally suddenly demanding and unpredictable in terms of the support they need from you.

One of the first things those dependent on you may think about is 'what does that mean for me?' What difference will your return to work make to their lives? Will it mean they have to do more about the house? Will they have to get used to other people looking after them and helping them with personal care, chores about the house, shopping etc?

Get people on board

It's important at this stage to get everyone on board, because you, about to undergo something of a change yourself, need all the support and positive thinking you can get – you don't need to be dragged down by worry or guilt. Make no bones about it: you deserve to go back to work, and to have a role in which you feel fulfilled and happy and are going to be successful.

Yes, people are going to have to make adjustments. They may need to find other people who are ready to help them out in an emergency, or do those little things you've been doing which has helped them out for so long. Yes, your siblings may have got used to you being the one who looks after your parents and doing everything. But remember:

> You've done your bit. It's time for the others to adjust to a change in their lives as much as you are about to create a change in yours.

Don't let them make you change your mind – you'll feel resentful and angry and it won't do your relationship any good. If they squeal, whine and moan, get help in from outside the family – your GP and Social Services will be a good place to start – but *don't* back-track. Once you've got a mind to return to work, you'll probably find you're looking forward to it and to abandon the idea won't make a happy outcome for you or anyone else.

Exercise

If you're feeling guilty about going back to work:

1. Add up all those hours you've given to the family and friends over the last year or six months. Write down *every single thing you've done and do* for them. And you'll be amazed at how long your list is. You've done your bit.

2. Write down all the benefits you and they will have as a result of you going back to work. A happier you, for a start.

If they start to object, show them the list, and simply comment *I've done my bit. I'm looking forward to a change.* It will show you're not a doormat and make them think.

Invest in a coach

However much we love our relatives and mates, they all have their own agenda. A coach will help you work to your agenda and not those of your family and friends. Find someone who will give you the impartial support and friendly motivation you need and who'll be there to give you a push when the going gets tough.

Tackling sweeping statements

According to your mother, Mrs Foggatt from Number 38 has spent six months looking for a job and has failed to find one. Your relatives are probably assuming that there are no jobs out there for people of Mrs Foggatt's age (similar to yours) or experience. They are putting negative and unhelpful thoughts into your mind by suggesting that it's going to be too difficult, too hard, and you'll feel down if you fail.

But ask yourself how much your relatives know about:

- The way Mrs Foggatt sold her skills and experience to prospective employers.
- How hard she really tried to find a job – may be she simply flicked through the local paper once a week.
- Whether she really researched every route back into the workplace – did she consider training programmes, for example?
- How far she targeted her search at companies which employed mature staff.
- Her real determination to get a job.

They probably won't have a clue.

> It's the process of job hunting and the attitude you take towards it that makes a difference to whether you're successful or not.

If comments people are making to you are really getting to you, ask yourself:

1. What they truly know about recruitment, employment, training and education opportunities.

2. What is making them so negative?
3. Ask them for details of successes. If they can't give you any, it shows how much experience they've got and what an unbalanced picture they have.
4. How much of what they are saying is fact and how much is hearsay? Where did they get their facts from?
5. What differences there were between the person they were talking about as their example and you? We're all unique and all have something different to bring to the workplace.

Are you really going to base your future on sweeping statements friends and family make? Find out their root, and you will usually find that they collapse like a deck of cards.

Looking at your partner's point of view

At best, your partner will wholeheartedly support your plans to return to work. However, he or she may have reservations about the whole thing, and it's important that you thrash those out, or they could become obstacles in your path, and hinder your progress.

Fears your partner may have include:

Will that mean more work for them?

This is especially the case if your partner is at full stretch already work-wise. Find solutions between you which will enable you to enjoy a sensible work–life balance such as:

- enlisting outside support with the house-work, i.e. hiring a cleaner, gardener, child-care support, sitters for your elderly relatives – whatever it takes;

- your partner investigating avenues for changing his or her working patterns, perhaps going from 100% full time to 75% full time. They may be very pleased to hear this idea!

Sit down together and work out your approach. Every couple is different, and the key is to find solutions that work for you and your needs and lifestyle preferences, rather than try to stick rigidly to prescribed answers in books.

How will you cope with emergencies?

Again, this is where you'll need strong support systems and back-up; be prepared to pay for these and have solutions at your finger tips, or in your mobile phone system so that you can implement them straight away. It's not for you to solve alone. Get your partner involved and get them to produce solutions as well. Find the one which works best of the occasion; there won't be any set rules or ways of dealing with things.

Will you change?

Yes, a return to work will change you. Any experience we go through in life changes us. Your exit from the workplace – for whatever reason – probably changed you as you went through new experiences and roles, but the fact is that you survived them and came through them. Point out some changes you've experienced together and remind your partner of the benefit changes bring. Find something new you can do together – something neither of you has ever done before. Enjoy the challenge together and laugh about it.

Will you still want them?

As you return to work, communication will be essential between you so that you can relate your experiences and how you're finding them and/or feeling about them. Show your partner that you still want them and that they are important to you by touching, kissing, holding hands, caressing, listening to what they are saying and building time into your week to have together doing something when the two of you have a chance to sit down and talk, listen, communicate, question, laugh and relax. Use your new-found income to enjoy a romantic break together or an evening out.

Their pride may suffer

If they've been the main breadwinner, their nose may be put out of joint. Don't you trust them anymore to bring the money in? Well, yes, you do, but going back to work isn't just about money, and in any case, it never hurt to have extra in the bank. Point out all the extra you can do with it – a reserve savings account for a rainy day, treats, breaks, a pension fund, a back-up in case they get made redundant or it happens to you.

Open them up to opportunity

This could provide a wonderful opportunity for them to change career or do something different, such as having time out. Ask them if they've ever thought they'd like a break, or to do something different. Your return to work could provide you all with the opportunity for them to do just that.

They don't want you to have any money of your own

They're a control freak! Some drastic change is needed in your relationship or you need to get out for your own wellbeing...

Whatever your partner's objections, have the facts to hand. Make a note of the time you've spent looking after the family and what the role has involved. They've probably never realised it and, once they do, they should welcome the opportunity for you to do something for yourself.

No experience?

It may be that you've never been employed before. The workplace may be a complete mystery to you, save what you've heard from the descriptions by friends, family and people you meet. Rather than planning a return to work, you may be thinking 'Time to go to work' or 'Time to start work'. There's plenty of help and support out there from colleges and training providers, government agencies and networks. Get your foot in the door; this may involve one of several steps depending on how confident you are and what your network is like:

- Picking up the phone and making an appointment with your local Jobcentre Plus to meet with an adviser.

- Making an appointment with a careers coach.

- Calling up a local college or training provider to see what courses they've got that can help you get into work – for example, many vocational courses include a period of work experience with sympathetic employers to give you a chance to show what you can do and put your theory into practice.

- Starting up your own business.

- Asking a friend to give you some work experience to see what really happens at work – try to get some in an area which interests you and which you think you'd enjoy.

Start with a simple action such as picking up the phone and watch your life take off from there.

You're never too old!

There's a lot of discussion about how difficult it is for older people (over 35 years old) to get a job. But many careers want mature people, and remember, you don't have to work for someone else. You can set up your own business and work for yourself.

The fact that there are more pieces of news about mature workers seeking opportunities in our press so often shows that people are aware something needs to change. Many companies are in fact showing themselves to be supporters of mature workers and taking them on. Study the image and values a company portrays when you're considering potential employers to apply to. Many will want to show that they have family values by representing all age groups and recruiting staff from the youngsters still at school to grandparents working at the till. More and more people are looking to work later in life to boost their pensions and companies are aware of that.

A bonus is that, as a mature person who has perhaps already had a family or got the travel lust out of your blood, you're less likely to disappear on maternity or paternity leave or to take off round the world for a year, leaving your employer to fill the gap. Stress your qualities such as reliability and maturity, and commitment to your next career move.

Much will depend on where you look for work, and how you market yourself. Talking about your grandchildren won't help you; talking about how well you relate to young people in their twenties and realising that you can learn from them as they can learn from you will.

Check out information for mature career changes

There are more and more avenues of information for those seeking a return to work or a change of career and more web sites dedicated to the older worker. These are listed at the back of the book.

Just out, now about

If you're returning to work after a spell in prison, you'll need to show you've adopted new strategies to help keep you on the right side of the law. With 20% of adults having a criminal record, you're not alone. Problems ex-offenders have when finding work include:

- Employer attitudes.
- Low self-esteem, confidence and motivation (see Chapter 10).
- Behavioural problems (see Further Reading).
- Poor health.
- Lack of qualifications and poor basic skills (see Chapter 9).
- Lack of informal contacts to help them find work (see Chapter 4).

If you think you have any of the above, take positive, active steps to tackle them. This book covers many of them. A survey by the Inner London Probation Service and the London Action Trust called *Who'd give me a job?* highlighted the need for offenders to declare convictions and reassure employers that their offending behaviour would not impinge on their work. Be honest and show potential employers that you do not present too great a risk. In particular, make sure your application is of the highest quality and get practice in interview technique.

Many employers are having problems recruiting suitably skilled and experienced people to vacancies, while unemployment rates are, at the time of writing, low. This should be good news for you. Most employers will take the nature of the crime into account on an individual basis, rather than baulking against ex-offenders as a whole. According to a report *Recruitment and Attitudes towards Ex-Offenders* produced by the Chartered Institute of Personnel and Development, 66% of human resource professionals who had employed ex-offenders reported that it had been a positive experience. Two thirds of human resource professionals interviewed thought it was reasonable to expect organisations to make a conscious effort to recruit ex-offenders.

- Make the most of the expertise and experience available in your local Jobcentre Plus and Probation Service to help you expand your network.

- Find out whether your local Learning and Skills Council is running any initiatives or programmes for ex-offenders in your area – there may be local projects up and running designed to help you.

- Call Learndirect to see what training and courses are on offer locally to boost your skills base.

- Get advice from your local National Association for the Care and Resettlement of Offenders (NACRO) office and organisations such as the Apex Trust.

- Consider joining training programmes and focus on making the most of the opportunities to build your experience and skills base.

- Use voluntary work as a way to show you have turned a corner and are on the road to honesty and reliability.

- Build up your network of contacts to help you secure work.

- Some people who've been on the wrong side of the law have successfully turned their negatives into positives by using the skills they acquired before they got into trouble to help people prevent crime.

- Sell yourself in as positive a light as possible, focusing on what you do well, your strengths and aspirations. Minimise the impact of your offence as much as you can and show that you have learnt from the experience. Show remorse.

- Talk to people you know who have returned to work. How did they find a job? What route did they take back to employment?

Frequently, employers want to help but just don't know how to start. If you meet someone who is interested in helping you but wants support, why not put them in touch with your Probation Office's team to help you get back on the road to employment?

Finally, if you are rejected, don't automatically assume it's because of your record. At the end of the day, there may have been other applicants who were a better fit for the role involved. They may have had a record too.

Using new strategies

If you remind yourself of what the benefits will be of returning to work, and have a clear picture of what you want to achieve in your mind and heart, the obstacles and barriers you face will diminish. Many of the obstacles truly facing us are those concerned with our own self-belief of what we are truly capable of – and the fact is that we are all capable of far more than we think.

Look for new routes to success

There are many different ways to achieve what you want – two fine examples are the number of different diets on the market to help people lose weight, or activities you can do to get fit. The point is, if one diet or form of exercise doesn't work, you stop doing it and give another one a go. And if you have to take a backward step one day in your journey to success, that doesn't mean you give up the following day. You simply look for a strategy which will work for you and be successful, and you use your determination and motivation to drive you to achieving that end goal, however long it takes.

The same is true if you're returning to work, or considering your career progression. There may be any number of ways for you to achieve what you want. You need to find a strategy which works in your sector – and if you're contemplating a change of career that could mean learning a new way you feel comfortable with. For example, some people will feel quite comfortable applying for jobs through an on-line agency. Others will be horrified at the thought.

Be alert to local initiatives, especially if you have special needs or circumstances. There are far more programmes now designed to help people back to work, so make the most of them.

Finally, think of strategies you haven't tried before. If all your old strategies are failing, why keep using them?

> Insanity is doing the same thing over and over again and expecting different results.   Albert Einstein

Do it now

- Remind yourself of the benefits of returning to work.
- Look at an obstacle or barrier you've overcome before. How did you handle it? What does that tell you about yourself?
- Listen in on people's conversations. Identify sweeping statements or generalisations you hear.
- Identify any barriers that might get in the way of your return to work and plot strategies to overcome them.

Summary

It's important to remember that many obstacles are more concerned with your own self-confidence, motivation and self-belief than any physical things people erect in your way.

- Think creatively about the ways 'barriers' can be overcome.

- Don't bulldoze through situations – think intelligently about how you can work through them.

- We have all got amazing power within us to do what we want. It's just that we forget it's there, or we were never told in the first place.

17

Managing the Return

Give yourself time to settle in and seek help where you need it.

Great! You've been offered the role you want, by letter or phone, or even at the interview! So what should you do now?

Landing the role, securing the deal

Before you do anything, take a couple of days to think about any offer you receive – don't be pressurised into accepting. If the person making the offer to you was in your shoes, they would want to do the same. Plus, it doesn't look good to appear desperate.

> Think before you sign: Are the organisation and role really what you want?

Ask yourself some searching questions

Questions to take into account before you accept an offer include:

1. How did you feel walking into the organisation?
2. Did it have a genuinely welcoming feel to it?
3. Is it the sort of place you'll actually look forward to going back to on a Monday morning? Did you get a good gut reaction to it?
4. Did you think *Yes, this is definitely for me – I'd love to work here?*
5. Have you found out the pros and cons of working for the organisation and how will the cons affect you and your daily working life?
6. Will you go places with the role and organisation? What might stop you?
7. Will the organisation enable you to achieve your career goals?

If your answers are all positive, then go for it! If not, you need to decide how much the negative parts will impact on your enjoyment of the role and career progression.

Deciding between two offers

You may be in the fortunate position of having to decide between two offers. There's always some hedging to be done while you try to decide which one to go for. You could write down the pros and cons of each offer and organisation, and see which one matches your needs, aspirations and values more closely than the other. And if you felt much happier in one organisation than the other, that should be telling you something. A gut feeling will tell you much; trust your instinct.

Dealing with all the formalities

You may have a number of formalities to go through and your offer may be dependent on some of them being satisfactory, such as:

- police checks
- medical report
- references
- your producing items such as certificates, driving licence, passport or anything the organisation requests.

Read through all the paperwork carefully and when you're sober – it does not do to enjoy a bottle of bubbly to celebrate the job offer and then whiz through the contract in a happy and alcoholic haze – you may miss something!

Sign the contract once you're happy and send it back with any documentation required with a covering letter to explain that you're looking forward to starting with the organisation. You may also need to sign a Confidentiality Agreement, which means that you promise to keep everything you see and hear relating to the business to yourself. You'll also need to make sure the company has details of the bank account you want your salary to be paid into, unless you are to be paid in cash. Give them your P45 so they can send it off to the tax office.

Starting out on day one

Prepare for your first day in advance, not on the morning you start. Decide what you're going to wear for the first few days (that's one thing less to think about in your first week), have a favourite meal ready for when you get home and something special to celebrate your first day. Check you've got petrol in the car, or your train ticket to hand, so that you don't have to queue. Take a mid-morning snack with you in case you're too nervous to eat any breakfast. Yes, this is all commonsense stuff – but it's so easily forgotten in the excitement and nervousness of that first day!

What to wear?

If you didn't take in what people wore when you went for an interview, go and watch people leave one day after work to get an idea of the dress code. If you're still in doubt, dress up rather than down. Once you've settled into the role, if your career aspirations are excited by what you're experiencing, watch what the next level up wear, and dress similarly to them. Dress for the role you want next, not for the one you're in!

Arriving

There's that awful arrival time, isn't there, where you feel everybody is watching you and wondering who you are! Most people remember what it's like to be new, but in the hustle and bustle of the working day, it may not seem like it. Be friendly and smile, smile, smile. No one will know how nervous you're feeling inside except you! Honest!

Asking questions is a good way to get to know people. You'll be full of enthusiasm and excited to be at your new workplace; in contrast, your new colleagues may not exude such happiness. Give the time needed to form working relationships with everyone – take part in anything you can, such as drinks in the pub after work, even if it's just a quick one, or walking to get a sandwich at lunch.

Dealing with your colleagues

Many firms recruit young people after their A levels or degrees on to management development programmes. They may be young enough to be your son or daughter and they may be your supervisor or boss. Remember – they are learning too!

Problem colleagues

If someone is upsetting you, try not to show it in public. Take a deep breath and count to ten. Look this person straight in the eye and sound in control. Remain cool and calm if you can. You've come a long way to get this position – you don't want to blow it all through a loss of temper or by handling things badly.

If this person is your superior and you feel their actions are unjustified – perhaps they are continually criticising you, bullying you or giving you far too much to do – take notes of the things they are doing to make your life a misery. Approach the problem in a constructive way. Ask for a meeting and go through the things they are doing well, and then give examples – a couple will do – of what they do that you don't enjoy. They may not even realise that they are upsetting you. Make sure you can give specific examples of what their behaviour is that you don't like and be clear how it affects you. If the problem persists, take it higher – but make sure you've got lots of evidence to back it up, so that you can be explicit.

Dealing with sexual harassment

If a colleague or client is making you feel very uncomfortable by their constant sexual innuendoes or comments, record every incident which upsets you. Note the day, time, what happened, and whether anyone else was there. Within your company, report the matter to your supervisor or human resources. You can, between you, then confront the guilty party about their behaviour. Outside of work, you can turn for help, advice and support to the Citizens Advice Bureau and the Equal Opportunities Commission. The alternative is to make a joke of their behaviour and scold the offending person as if they were a child. But never, ever be alone with them in the office after everyone else has gone.

Working with email and the Internet

Many employees use the email for personal reasons, to gossip, send saucy emails and organise their social life. Some email message lists resemble the advice columns in magazines. Some companies access their staff's email messages to see how many of them are personal. Make sure you know and abide by your company's email and Internet policy and, if you manage or supervise staff, familiarise yourself with it quickly. Talk to other managers to see how they handle email and Internet misuse. Many companies have a policy of instant dismissal if email and Internet are used in appropriately.

Enjoying the office party

Go, relax and enjoy, and have a great time. Even if the drink is free, don't get wildly drunk. Your behaviour may be noted. Watch how others behave and aim to be slightly better than them!

Getting social

Many organisations have social and sports clubs or outings to boost team morale and encourage staff to get to know each other. These provide excellent opportunities for you to network and raise your profile in your own right.

Contributing to the organisation

You know how much you appreciate it if someone goes the extra mile for you. You sit up and think, *I'm going to use that company again*. Business is very much about showing an interest in your clients' affairs and a willingness to help them solve problems and do well. It's about building relationships with your customers and helping them through the tough times and the good.

Hence the reason it is important to recruit people who are professional and really take pride in their work, who are passionate about doing it well and helping others. Even if you are 'just' a check-out operator, your attitude and the way you greet your customers makes an impact.

> People judge a company very much on the attitude and performance of its staff.

Every single person in an organisation has responsibility for its growth and reputation, and for attracting new customers and retaining existing ones.

Meeting deadlines

Excelling in business isn't just about smiling and showing a caring face to customers. It's also very much about delivering quality products and services when you say you will. If you call a company for information and it doesn't arrive within a day or so, you start to feel that the company is letting you down and that they don't really care whether you receive the information or not. That organisation has failed to deliver.

Exercise

Getting the job done and anticipating a customer's needs are an integral part of excellent service.

1. As you are served by staff over the next few weeks in any capacity, think about the service you are given. Rank the standard. How could the member of staff have gone further in meeting your expectations?

2. Think back to the last time you were served by someone who didn't care what you thought of the service. What impression did this give you of their company? Did you go back, given that you had a choice of companies to choose from? Or did you choose to take your business elsewhere?

3. Knowing how you reacted, what can you do at work which will make a difference to the way in which customers view your business or organisation?

Performance review and appraisals

Many companies give their staff reviews and appraisals. These help staff set goals and identify any training needs they may have in order to achieve them. Staff may receive bonuses depending on their results and/or a team may be rewarded for its performance, or the whole company for the year's efforts.

Performance review and appraisals help you to focus on what your job involves and how it is changing and contributing to the organisation and team, and what sorts of skills and competences you will need to acquire to cope with future changes. A review will help you identify whether you are doing your job well and how you might do it more effectively than at present.

Prepare well for your review – it is a great chance to talk about where you want your career to go with the organisation and to secure any training you need to do a great job.

Continuing to learn

The workplace changes fast, thanks to research which brings us new products and services, new social trends and attitudes, and political, economic and legislative developments. It's important to keep learning and training – but also to know how to get the information you need as and when you need it.

Keep training and learning

The ways you learn and train at work will depend on the needs of your employer and the way in which they operate. Companies may train you by all or some of the following methods:

- On the job training – learning by doing.
- Secondment.
- Evening courses.
- In-house training done by trainers employed by the company or brought in for that purpose.
- Correspondence courses.
- National vocational qualifications.
- Day release courses, i.e. one day a week at college, the other four at work.
- Role play.
- Video and feedback.
- Study for academic qualifications.
- Giving presentations.
- Work shadowing.
- Mentoring and coaching.
- On-line.

Many employers now have facilities for learning with dedicated learning PC facilities or an Intranet. Some develop partnerships with local training providers, universities and colleges to bring in the expertise in training and development they need. Larger companies are likely to have their own training sections, but smaller ones may simply rely to an 'as and when' approach.

Keep track of all your learning

It shows you're motivated and enthusiastic and keen on progressing your career.

> Every time you do something new, you are building your skills and confidence.

Be prepared to train in your own free time

You may want to boost your capabilities in a particular area which is different to that your company wants you go to in. Be willing and ready to study at college to further your portfolio of skills in your own free time. You can always take your newly-acquired skills elsewhere. The Internet has a vast selection of helpful information, including ways to fund your training.

Continuing Professional Development

Many professions demand CPD (as it is known) as part of the responsibilities involved in being a member. This is particularly true in any area where there are going to be huge changes, such as architecture, surveying, banking and financial services, medicine and dentistry. Customers expect those servicing them to be up to date in their knowledge and skills and so the staff needs to continue training. In some sectors, where new regulations have been enforced, staff who have been doing the job for some considerable time may still be required to prove that their competence and knowledge are up to date by studying for and taking examinations. As their customer, you'd expect nothing less.

Many professions also expect you to take up membership of their association and/or to study for examinations it has set. This is done in order to maintain the standards set by that body so that the public can have confidence in its members. If you were to call out a plumber, you'd want him or her to know what they were doing, wouldn't you? A professional qualification and membership of the professional body signals that the tradesperson has met the standards required.

Some professional bodies give their members useful benefits, such as special prices on insurance, so it's always worth getting in touch to see what's in it for you. This is the case whether you're employed with a company or self-employed. Some companies will pay for your professional membership, and you should check with the Inland Revenue to see if you can put your membership fees down on your tax form to reclaim them as part of your business.

Do it now

- Visualise how your week will look once you go back to work. What will you fit in when? What will you have to change once you go back?
- What back-up plans can you bring into play for those nights you feel tired and don't feel like cooking?
- Sit down with your partner or a friend and plan a treat or outing you'll both enjoy at the end of your first month or week at work.

Summary

Going back to work will change your life and it may take time to adjust. So:

- Be kind to yourself.

- Get plenty of fresh air and exercise in the evenings or by going out for a walk at lunch time or at weekends.

- Plan lots of stress-free activities which will enable you to relax outside of working hours.

18

Managing Life, Work and Fun

6Life is not a dress rehearsal. It's for living today!9

It's all very well having a super new job, but if life outside work is causing you grief, then that's going to impinge on your working life. Once you've been back in work for three months, take a good look at your life overall and see if you need to make some changes to give yourself the lifestyle you want and truly deserve.

Buying yourself time

Most of us would dearly love to have more time. You can manage time (and energy, usually) by streamlining the way you work and taking a long hard look at everything you do and what, out of that list, you don't need to do or could delegate or outsource. For example, you could outsource your cleaning, ironing and gardening. Life is too short to be spent over an ironing board, unless you enjoy ironing.

Get a wall planner

Available from any stationers, put a year planner on the wall in your home where all the family can see and make good use of it. Coloured stickers can be used to denote various activities or family members, whatever works best for you. Get everyone into the routine of putting their dates up fast. Put up all the dates which are important to you, including family holidays, birthdays, check-ups with the dentist and vet, school terms – anything you can do which will save you having to find the date in your memory. Similarly, display a list of phone numbers beside the wall chart so that you don't have to waste time looking them up. You can then negotiate with your employer to take time out for any important dates.

Say no

Start saying 'no'. Too many of us say 'yes, yes, yes' all the time, be it to our kids who want us to be the taxi service or friends who want to drop in unexpectedly when we feel more like enjoying some peace. We've lost the art of restraint, so start using it again and life will get easier and less stressful. Don't be a doormat.

Streamline your systems

Look at ways in which you can save yourself time by:

- Paying bills by Direct Debit each month, rather than writing cheques.
- Using the Internet to do supermarket shopping and then buying what you can in bulk.
- Cooking double the amount you need for one meal and freezing half.
- Keeping the numbers of delivery food suppliers so that you can order your meal in time for your arrival home.

Getting the kids to do some of the housework – it will prepare them well for the day they leave home. Make life too comfortable, and they never will. So they say they're too busy? If they've got time to play computer games, watch TV and socialise, then they've got time to help.

Looking after yourself

If you're finding things stressful:

- Reduce the amount of caffeine, alcohol and cigarettes you consume.
- Treat yourself to a massage as often as you can afford it.
- Go to bed incredibly early one night of the week with a good book and take the phone off the hook.
- Get plenty of exercise.
- Make sure there's lots of laughter and fun in your life.
- Field calls at home with an answer phone.

The key is to identify what stresses you out, and then to find tackle ways to deal with it. Fast!

Business versus family life

Don't be surprised if, once you start, business ignores your family life, whatever promises were made to you at interview. In fact, if you *expect* the business to ignore family life, you'll be in for less of a shock. Get back-up plans for your family so that you're absolutely covered in the event you have to work late or go into work at weekends.

Prioritise what is important to you

Be clear about what is important to you after you've finished work for the day and keep checking to see if your priorities are changing. You may find you haven't got the time you once had to see friends but then there may also be people you don't want to stay in touch with whom you'd happily have an excuse to see less of.

Making time for you

Don't be surprised if, when you get home from work, you need half an hour or so to unwind and just be quiet. If you allow yourself to be run ragged, you'll end up exhausted, stressed and ill. Take time out to do whatever you enjoy doing. Give yourself full permission to slump in sloppy clothes in front of the TV with a packet of nibbles and a glass of wine. Buy that bar of chocolate and munch it without feeling guilty. Have a face pack as you soak in the bath. If you find this sort of thing difficult to fit into the day, schedule an appointment with yourself. You'll feel much better for it, and those living with you will benefit too!

Gone back after an illness?

If you're finding it hard to cope, talk to your line-manager or human resources. Is it possible you could do work from home, change your hours, reduce your hours or alter your responsibilities for a while? Talk to your occupational health nurse your organisation has one.

Changing relationships

As we go through changes in our lives, so we change and grow. You may find that the experiences you've had since have altered your views, perceptions, behaviour, attitude, approach and confidence. You're a new person, with a new daily routine, friends, responsibilities, opportunities, knowledge and interests. Your old friends and relatives may well have stayed the same. They may be trying to hook up to the new you and finding it tough.

> Make time for your friends and family. They will help you keep things in perspective and keep you refreshed.

Think of things you can do with friends that will minimise the amount of work and maximise the enjoyment and fun you'll have. Why not agree to meet up at a pub, rather than have someone slave over a hot stove? Or go on a picnic, or out for a walk? There's no substitute for fresh air, exercise, good food, fun and laughter to keep the stress levels down and to boost your sense of well-being.

Spend time with your partner

Build time into the week to do things together. Do activities which are fun and make you laugh and – crucially – talk openly and honestly. Your partner may be having successes, worries or difficulties with their own career, so be a good listener and motivator. If you need to, give someone else a job and buy yourself time by outsourcing activities such as housework and gardening, grocery shopping on-line and even using a lifestyle manager or virtual PA to get those tasks done that you find tiresome.

Set goals for the year together

Set your own individual goals but aim for something the two of you can do *together*. Take the example of a couple whose kids had left home. They decided that every month they would do something together they had never done before. So far, they've gone hot air ballooning, had a romantic weekend away, tried a new restaurant, been abseiling and taken a local history course. The extra money Angela is earning is helping to pay for these monthly treats, and they are relishing their new experiences together.

Some ideas for goals you could set together include:

- A major holiday to an exotic destination.
- Putting money into an extra savings account for retirement.
- Learning a new language together.
- Buying a new car.

- Buying a dinghy.
- Taking up a new hobby you can enjoy together.
- Renewing your wedding vows and going on another honeymoon.

Keep talking

Find time to talk, and do activities which give you the opportunity to do this when neither of you are tired or stressed, and which don't involve alcohol. Alcohol lessens our judgement, so if you've got a sensitive issue which needs to be aired, it's not a wise move to do it after you've downed a bottle of wine together.

Relationships are like careers: if you don't invest time and energy, attention and care into them, they wilt and stop growing. Give them the time and energy, focus and love they deserve, and you'll enjoy far greater personal happiness at work and at home.

What are you tolerating?

We all put up with things in life that we don't particularly enjoy. We can't do anything about some of them. But we spend a great deal of time moaning about things we can do something about. These things get in the way of our making the most of our time, energy, focus, health and enjoyment. Do any of the below tolerations in life sound familiar to you? They are examples and you may be able to think of more:

- Not saying 'no' often enough (to friends and family, as much as employers) ☐

- Poor sleep patterns ☐

- Health problems you're not getting to the root of ☐

- Friends who drain of you of your time and energy ☐

- Family who don't play their part in looking after elderly relatives – they expect you to make the phone calls, do the visiting, sort out their lives ☐

- Financial debts and worries ☐
- Being disorganised ☐
- A relationship which drags you down – it could be friend or partner ☐
- Faulty equipment that needs mending ☐
- Lack of fitness ☐
- Too much reliance on substances such as alcohol, comfort food, cigarettes to get you through the day ☐
- Spending too much time watching rubbish on television ☐
- Gambling ☐
- Lack of confidence ☐
- Spending too much time worrying about things you cannot do anything about ☐
- Moaning about something instead of doing something about it ☐
- Shyness in social situations ☐
- Spending too much time surfing the Net ☐

You're putting up with a lot of tolerations or things that are interfering with your enjoyment and effectiveness in life. So:

1. Identify what effect anything you've ticked above is having on your life.
2. What would your life be like if you got rid of them?
3. Ask yourself how long you've been putting up with them.
4. How much longer are you prepared to put up with them?
5. What could you do to get rid of them and tackle them once and for all?
6. What are you going to spend the time and energy on after you've got rid of them?

Now identify what you're actually going to do and when. Get supporters on-side – people who'll help and support you. Be prepared for those tolerations and interferences to try to come back into your life. Stamp on them fast!

Tolerations and interferences at work

These impact at work too! Examples include:

- Gossiping (other people, not you!).
- Lack of organisation.
- Information overload.
- Mishandling of emails.
- Meetings.
- Lack of communication and understanding.
- Not understanding your role and responsibilities.
- Lack of direction from your manager.
- Sloppiness and making mistakes.

There's a fine line between building working relationships at work and taking part in the social aspects of it; and spending too much time gossiping. Your own judgement will help you work out what is right for the culture and company you're in. When you start, it's important to take part in social events to get to know people, even if it's just going to the pub for a drink at lunchtime or after work.

Immunise yourself against bugs

Interferences come between you and your enjoyment of life and performance in it. Below are simple steps to tackle them:

1. Be aware they exist.
2. Watch for them creeping into your life, work, body, heart and soul.
3. Tackle them.
4. Ensure they've gone away and won't come back.

Getting support

As you go back to work you may want support, even if it's just someone to talk to from time to time. There are plenty of support groups out there, so make the most of them. You could find yourself becoming a volunteer and getting involved in helping others further down the line – you never know.

So assess what you need:

- Is it a listening ear? ☐
- Reassurance you're doing the right thing? ☐
- Practical help with someone you care for? ☐
- Time out for you a couple of times a week? ☐
- More flexibility from your employer in terms of the hours and way you work? ☐
- The opportunity to talk through a situation with someone? ☐
- The chance to talk to someone who's been in a similar situation – you need to know you're not alone. ☐
- Help and advice on a particular problem? ☐
- A break from caring for someone for a weekend so you can get away or catch up? ☐
- A mentor whom you can turn to for advice? ☐
- Someone to help you stay on the straight and narrow? ☐
- Some laughter in your life? ☐
- Other? _____

Then find the relevant group. You can do this by searching on the Internet, of course, but don't forget people such as your GP, church and social services, all of whom have strong networks throughout the community.

When you find the right group, make the most of the experience and expertise they have to offer. Sometimes you will need to rummage around for this, be it on the Internet, on their web site or on the telephone. Once you mention your problem or situation, you'll be astounded at how many people come out and are ready to talk to you about it.

> Laughter and humour are important weapons in the fight against stress, so don't forget them.

Handling emergencies

If you cannot go to work because you are ill, speak to your immediate boss to let them know, or leave them a voice-mail. Bosses are suspicious of messages passed through friends in the company – it doesn't look good, and anyway, you may need to discuss things that may crop up while you're off sick. Many organisations are open plan now, so if you're suffering from a bug, it may well be better to stay away until you really are recovered, as bugs spread quickly round open-plan air-conditioned offices. Stay home and don't go back to work until you're fully fit.

If you are a carer, find out if there is a Carers Emergency Scheme in your area. This is a single contact number with an operator who can put a pre-arranged emergency plan you have devised into action. Carry details with you of emergency social services teams, emergency respite and sitting services and have an alarm fitted in the home of any elderly relatives or people you care for. Keep numbers on you of people such as their GP (normal and out of hours services), any day care centres they attend, relatives, friends and neighbours who can help out and make sure they all have details of the person's medication, condition, likes and dislikes, and relevant contact numbers.

Dealing with family illness

No matter how well you prepare for the eventuality, the day will come when your working life is disrupted for a family crisis, so:

- Make sure it really is a crisis and that whoever is calling you for help isn't just testing you to see if you drop everything and run. Go into work later and leave early if you have to, but make it in if you can.

- Find out whether anyone from your support network could help you out, even if it's just for an hour while you get some work from the office and pop home. You could still get calls at home from work or take a lap top to help you get things done.

- If you need to be absent, speak to you boss.

Try to arrange a system with your partner so that you take it in turns to be off, or something similar. It isn't fair for one of you to continually drop everything and hold the fort.

Dealing with long-term sickness

A member of your family falls ill and the responsibility falls to you to look after them. Many employers are very sympathetic in such circumstances, and it's worth trying to keep going. Working may provide the break you really need if you're at home most of the time looking after someone, and the companionship and gossip will take your mind off things.

What help is available?

Talk to Social Services about possible support they can offer. They will need to assess both your needs and those of the person you care for, but they may be able to offer services such as:

- Direct support e.g. a day care centre or care in the home.

- Direct payments so that you can buy your own support.

- Giving you details of registered and approved private care facilities.

- Information of national and local groups who can help.

You may be eligible for the carer's allowance and other benefits, so give the Department for Work and Pensions a call (see Useful Addresses) to find out more.

Even if you have to pay for someone to pop in, at least they will give you the break you'll need, probably more than you realise. It may be possible for you to work from home, going into the office once or twice a week for team meetings.

Find out what support your employer can offer

Talk to your human resources department, welfare or occupational health adviser, union or staff representative and colleagues to find out what support your employer offers. If your company has no policy on help to employees, why not suggest a group of you get together and formulate one? If you need to take time out again to look after someone or care for yourself, think of ways in which you can continue working, such as going part-time, job-sharing, working from home and reducing your hours. If this is not possible, ask about options such as a career break, voluntary redundancy or early retirement.

> Employers don't want to lose highly committed, motivated quality staff. They want to keep them.

Do it now

- Identify what's changed about you since you started work. How do you feel about your future in the workplace now?

- Talk to your partner about the way things are going since you returned to the workplace. Are you both happy with the way things are working out? If not, what can you do to improve the situation?

- Plan to do something which celebrates your return to work!

Summary

Going back to work can be tiring and stressful so you need to look after yourself. If you can't take care of number one, you can't take care of anyone else properly.

- Build time into your day for you, and for your partner and you.
- Watch for any interferences in your life which prevent you from living it to the full.
- Be prepared for problems at home and have strategies to handle them.

19

Creating Change

6Create change and be alert to change. Make opportunities out of it.9

Change is a hot topic. Courses are delivered on it, books written about it, presentations and lectures given around it. Your ability to handle change and be comfortable with it will help you to enjoy life and make the most of it.

A changing world

Change is taking place in a number of ways:

- *Global* – from the terrorist attack on 11 September 2001 to the tsunami in Asia at the end of 2004, change is global and affecting us all and the way we live our lives.
- *Legislative and regulatory* – from those created by your town council and Parliament, to the European Union and the speed camera down the road.

- *Fast* – the speed with which new IT equipment is being introduced is frightening. The PC you buy today is old hat tomorrow.

- *Knowledge* – knowledge is rapidly becoming outdated thanks to research and development. An example is the new treatments being developed to treat illnesses such as cancer and heart problems.

- *Personal* – changes imposed on us, such as redundancy, illness or death of a family member or friend; or chosen by us, such as marriage, parenthood, moving to live abroad, career changes.

- *Attitudes and expectations* – as customers, we have increasingly high standards of customer service and products and goods and services. So far as our own lives go, we know we can make changes happen, if we have the necessary 'get up and go' required.

- *Competitiveness* – the world has become an increasingly competitive place, especially at work, as organisations seek to be the Number One choice for customers.

Change can have a huge impact on individuals, and make a person feel even smaller and less influential in any given situation. Change can hit home hard and personally, but remember that it can be beneficial too. But change brings with it responsibilities and demands for our own willingness to adapt, learn and move with the times.

Creating and responding...your organisation

Organisations have a huge job creating change and responding to it, but a lot of them fail to point out why changes are taking place or to spell out clearly enough what the benefits of change will be to staff. Such a lack of control can be particularly frustrating if you've been in charge of your daily routine and life for some time. Remember that the world is changing, so your organisation needs to reflect that change. Its customers will be changing their needs, demands, attitudes, views and approaches. Thanks to research and development, customers can buy an increasingly diverse range of products through different means using various payment methods. Their shareholders and owners will expect good returns on their investments, so organisations will constantly be looking to find the fastest, most cost-effective route to carrying out their missions.

Don't expect others to stay around

One of the things you may notice is that people join and leave an organisation very quickly these days. They are very much looking after their own career development and, if the company they're working for isn't providing what they want, they are tending to up sticks and move to one that will. You may join a firm and have a new boss only to find several months later that she or he has gone and someone else taken their place. That departure could happen very suddenly, especially if the organisation works in a particularly competitive sector.

Changing roles

In the old days, personnel officers laboriously wrote out carefully drafted job descriptions to which people rigidly adhered. Everyone knew what they had to do and stuck to that and there was a huge hierarchy with a formal atmosphere. That was acceptable, because the world wasn't changing at the speed it is now.

Today, although job descriptions exist outlining the specific duties and responsibilities of the job holder, employees have to be willing to do more than their job description says. In a fast changing world, job descriptions are too rigid. Consequently, companies want to take on people who welcome and cope positively with change, who are adaptable and flexible. Those who dislike and fear change will find life difficult. The more you are able to embrace change, the better you will be able to cope with it.

If your organisation is constantly changing, it follows that your role should be too. Are you developing the skills you need to do well the job you're doing? Are you in touch with what's going on in your sector, what the threats, weaknesses are facing your department and company? What are the opportunities and strengths that you have, your department has and your company?

> Be alert to opportunities – inside your new employing organisation and outside it.

Knowing when to move on is an essential skill in life today. Many people stay in the same role, when they know it's time something changed but they remain as they are and become increasingly frustrated and uninterested in what they are doing.

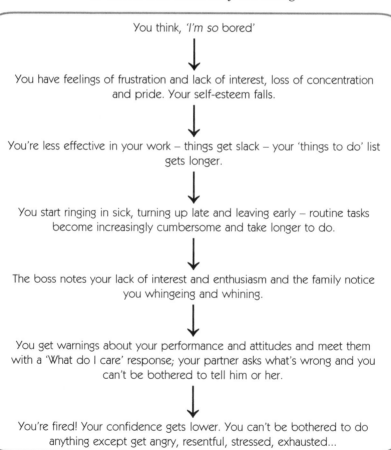

Figure 16: Knowing when it's time to move on.

 **Constantly employed**

With the exception of parenthood, the days of a job for life are over. Organisations themselves cannot control many of the things happening today, so they certainly can't control your career with any degree of stability. You have to take control of it yourself; the responsibility is yours.

Any job will, if a company is moving forward, change without the aid of a job description. Those who are not willing to learn new skills and take on new projects stand to jeopardise their employability.

Stay aware

It's easy to be blind to the changes that are taking place at work when you're in the middle of the usual hustle and bustle of telephones, emails, meetings and demands customers and your colleagues make on your energy and time.

Exercise

Take yourself away from your desk, mentally, and imagine filming yourself and your colleagues at work.

1. What is happening to your company? Is your department under threat, perhaps by being merged with another one, and are redundancies likely?

2. What could you do to boost your effectiveness and contribution, both as an individual and as a department?

3. What would you do if you were made redundant?

Keep a high profile

Network in your organisation. Talk to people you don't know; find out who they are and what they do. Join committees, take part in social events. Put forward well thought-out ideas and solutions to problems. Find ways to save the company money and time. Expand your skills in the company's time and your own. Take on a project or responsibility in your own right, which will enable you to work with others across the organisation in different departments.

As your confidence back at work grows and your abilities become clear, you'll find yourself in a strong position to take advantage of the opportunities that exist – but you need to show you're ready for them by exhibiting the right behaviour, attitude and approach expected of someone who is going to be moving on up. A mentor can be particularly useful, if you want to progress, as someone who's been there, done it and got the T-shirt, and can help you plot your career progression in territory he or she knows and understands well.

The sky's the limit

The world is your oyster. The golden question is, how far do you want to go? It's difficult to know what will happen to you when you get back to work. What may have started out as a gentle job to bring in extra cash may suddenly unleash a passion to really make it all happen and test yourself to the utmost. Review what you want to achieve in life regularly so that you can make the most of it. 'If only!' and 'too late' are the two saddest phrases in the English language.

Much will depend on what is important to you. We all have our own values. Your boss may be anxious to be in charge in five years' time and expect her team to perform to such an extent that it will boost her chances of acquiring such a golden award. She may be tough and unforgiving as a result. You may prefer to have a happier balance of life and work.

Ask yourself:

- Where do I want to be in five years' time?
- What do I need to do to make that happen?
- What will my life be like once I achieve it?
- What will I need to sacrifice en route to make it happen?
- What will happen if I don't make it happen?
- What will I feel like if I succeed? And if I don't?

There are various routes open to you to make what you want happen in work. You could choose any of the following routes:

- Progressing with your own company – onwards and upwards.
- Changing company to make the next important move happen.
- Setting up on your own.

Much depends on the balance you and yours want in life and how much of a role you want work to play and how much it figures in your idea of a successful and happy life.

Re-write your CV regularly

Re-write your CV every year, even if you are in the same post, and even if you're running your own business. This exercise will show you how far you're progressing and in which direction, because you can add your achievements to it in terms of new qualifications, responsibilities, skills, and the contribution you've made. Expand your CV to include things which you did and got involved with outside of work, as well, so that you can take into account how much you did in life, as opposed to work.

Consider how your CV looks different from the previous version. If you sit back and think, *Wow, what a year* and feel proud, and like celebrating, that's great. If looking at it makes you feel, *Well, I didn't do very much this year,* then ask yourself why and how much that matters to you. Maybe you had to tackle family emergencies or devoted time to a new hobby. You may have boosted your skills and confidence in handling difficult people if family members have been difficult; or perhaps you've suffered a bereavement. Take a human view of your past year, and take a holistic approach and look at your life overall.

Consider what you'd like to change in your life next year. You may say, *Nothing – I'm happy with the way things are.* That's fine, but take a closer look. Is there anything you'd like to introduce to your life, or spend less time on? Perhaps you'd like to see less of some friends or more of others. Examine every area of your life carefully before you declare yourself satisfied.

Keep an up-to-date copy of a CV ready at home, two pages long, for the purpose of finding a new job. An opportunity may suddenly come your way, either for your current company (an internal move, a promotion, perhaps), or a client could put in a good word for you to someone he knows in a similar business. Of course, you may turn such opportunities down, but it's nice to be asked and to be ready to consider them swiftly and decisively.

Remembering the benefits of change

It's easy to forget the benefits things we do bring us, especially if it takes a while to start, undertake and conclude the process. It's like deciding to get fit; the more you remind yourself of the benefits that fitness will bring you, the more motivated you will be and the more likely you are to achieve your goal. When times get tough, that's when you need to focus on what you end goal is and what it will feel like when you get there and achieve it.

Exercise

It's easy to forget the benefits that change has brought. Take a moment to list all the good things which have happened to you as a result of returning to work. Yes, income will be one. But there are plenty more, such as confidence, belief in your own ability. You'll be a much stronger person as a result of having done it.

Celebrating – life's too short not to!

I need to make changes!

That's great! Identify the changes you want exactly and how you're going to make them happen. Push back those boundaries – the more you do, the more you'll feel like doing. And that applies too, if you just claimed you're happy with the way things are, thank you very much.

Securing your future

A regular SWOT analysis will help you determine how secure you are, whether you're self-employed or working for someone else. Get your partner to do one too, so that the two of you can work out any gaps, for example, in your financial position, and work to fill them in. It's a great way to show you how great a team you are, or, if you're not feeling very much like a team, to start building a stronger relationship.

S   Identify the Strengths you have and ways in which you can build on them.

W Know your Weaknesses. How can you overcome them?

O Identify Opportunities out there for you to strengthen your position and make your goals happen.

T   Threats – know what might threaten your security, happiness and well-being. Then protect yourself.

You can do this exercise in any area of your life, from your health to your finances, home to work. Assessing your current position regularly helps you identify problems early on and build up a strong feeling of well-being. Once you've done a SWOT analysis, identify actions to take such as:

1. Studying for a qualification to give you extra skills to offer an employer;
2. Meeting with an independent financial adviser who can identify products which can fill any gaps in your financial provision;
3. Build up a reserve of three to six months' living expenses in your bank account as soon as you can.
4. Booking in for a complete MOT medical from head to toe. Your car has an annual MOT, so why shouldn't you?
5. Analysing your time to ensure that you're not wasting valuable minutes on things or people you'd rather not be dealing with; and smoothing out your procedures for handling areas such as tax, insurance, the car and so forth at home.

Case study: Kevin, Owner of Outdoor Pursuits Store

'In my line of work, I need to know what the latest products are so that I can stock them. I need to be aware of customer demands at certain times of the year, to keep up with all the latest things on the market. I need to know what position my company has in the market; I cater for the professional and serious outdoor enthusiast, rather than the Sunday camper. I'm constantly reading the trade magazines, in touch with my customers to find out what they want, and going on outdoor pursuits myself to test my equipment so I know what the new stuff can do. Yes, it takes time to keep up to date, but that's what my customers expect.'

Do it now

- Write down your career goals for the next year. What do you want to do and achieve? What will you need to do to make that happen and who will help you?
- Be clear about what achieving those goals will mean for you and those close to you.
- Write down how you are feeling about this new change in your life – going back to work. What does it tell you about yourself and life?
- Celebrate! You've done it! You've gone back to work!

Summary

Remember that change has its benefits. Know where you are going in life and what you want to get out of it, and those changes imposed on you will be easier to handle.

- Don't waste time and energy worrying about those changes we cannot do anything about.
- Celebrate change; life would be so much duller without it.

Further Reading

Job hunting

Great Answers to Tough Interview Questions, Martin John Yate
   (Kogan Page)
How to Master Psychometric Tests, Mark Parkinson (Kogan Page)
How to Pass Selection Tests, Sanjay Modha and Mike Byron (Kogan
   Page)
Succeeding at Interviews, Judith Verity (How To Books)
The Job Application Handbook, Judith Johnston (How To Books)
The Ultimate Job Search Letters Book, Martin Yate (Kogan Page)
Write a Great CV, Paul McGee (How To Books)

Careers

Occupations, published annually by COIC and available in libraries
   and bookshops
Surfing Your Career, H. Nickell (How To Books)
The Times A-Z of Careers and Jobs, Irene Krechowieckza (Kogan
   Page)
The 100 Greatest Ideas for Building Your Career, Ken Langdon
   (Capstone Publishing)
Your Rights at Work, TUC Guide (Kogan Page)

Self-employment

Going for Self-Employment, John Whiteley (How To Books)
How I Made It: 40 Successful Entrepreneurs Reveal All, Rachel

Bridge (Kogan Page)

How to Choose A Franchise, Iain Murray (Kogan Page in association with *The Daily Express*)

Starting Your Own Business, Jim Green (How To Books)

Start and Run Your Own Business, Alan Le Marinel (How To Books)

Successful Marketing for the Small Business, Dave Patten (Kogan Page)

The Ultimate Business Plan, Phil Stone (How To Books)

The 100 Greatest Ideas for Making Money on the Internet, Ros Jay (Capstone Publishing)

100 Ways to Make Your Business A Success, Neil Bromage (How To Books)

Education

Learning How to Study Again, Dr Catherine Dawson (How To Books)

The Mature Students' Guide to Higher Education, available from UCAS (see Useful Addresses) free of charge

Student Money Matters, supported by UCAS, published by Trotman & Co

University and College Entrance: The Official Guide available from bookshops or in your local library, published annually

What Do Graduates Do? published annually by AGCAS in association with UCAS and CSU

Higher Education and Disability: The Guide to Higher Education for People with Disabilities, available from Skill (See Useful Addresses) for a fee

Social entrepreneurship

The New Alchemists: How Visionary People Make Something out of Nothing by Charles Handy, The Random House Group, 1999

Go for it!

Boost Your Self-Esteem, John Caunt (Kogan Page)
Build Your Own Brand, Eleri Sampson (Kogan Page)
Feel the Fear and Do It Anyway, Susan Jeffers (Arrow Books)
Increasing Confidence, Philippa Davies (Dorling Kindersley)

Life

Get Everything Done and Still Have Time To Play, Mark Forster (Hodder & Stoughton)
Goals: How To Get Everything You Want – Faster Than You Ever Thought Possible, Brian Tracey (Berrett-Koehler Publishers Inc)
Moving On Up: Inspirational Advice to Change Your Life, Edited by Sarah Brown (Ebury Press: The Random House Group)
Take Time For Your Life, Cheryl Richardson (Bantam Books)
The Luck Factor: Change your Luck and Change Your Life, Dr Richard Wiseman (Century: Random House Group)
What Should I Do With My Life? Po Bronson, (Vintage: The Random House Group)

Future focused

Your Retirement Masterplan, Jim Green (How To Books)

Useful Addresses

Department for Education and Skills. Helpline: 0870 000 2288
www.dfes.gov.uk The Adult Learners gateway has lots of information on courses at every level and on financing them.

Department for Employment and Learning, Student Support Branch,
39–49 Adelaide Street, Belfast BT2 8FD. Tel: 0289 025 7777 or
visit *www.deni.gov.uk*

Student Awards Agency for Scotland, Gyleview House, 3 Redheughs
Rigg, Edinburgh EH12 9HH, Tel: 0131 476 8212 or visit
www.student-support-saas.gov.uk

Careers Scotland – provides a comprehensive, co-ordinated and free
guidance service for people of any age in Scotland at
www.careers-scotland.org.uk

Learning and Skills Councils – find yours and see what it has to offer
at *www.lsc.gov.uk*. Look for the Adult Learner pages or call 0870
900 6800. Information, Advice and Guidance Partnerships are
funded by LSCs to provide information, advice and guidance to
adults 20 and over about learning and work opportunities.

IAG: Visit *www.myiag.org* which will enable you to find an
Information, Advice and Guidance Partnership in your area.

Learndirect. Free confidential impartial service offering information
and advice on learning opportunities and careers. You can find out
information on courses throughout the UK, take Learndirect's own
courses on-line and talk through your careers ideas with a Lifelong
Learner. Helpline: 0800 100 900 (0808 100 9000 in Scotland) or
visit *www.learndirect.co.uk*

The National Association of Educational Guidance for Adults
(NAEGA), has a directory of organisations providing adult
educational and career guidance. Visit www.naega.org.uk for

further details.

www.worktrain.gov.uk – a tremendous web site with lots of links through to information on training, employment, opportunities, voluntary work and funding for training. Also links to professional bodies.

Education

Association of British Correspondence Colleges, PO Box 17926, London SW19 3WB. Tel 020 8544 9559. Will send out a brochure with information about courses and colleges available or visit *www.homestudy.org.uk*

British Dyslexia Association, 98 London Road, Reading, RG1 5AU. Tel 0118 966 8271, *www.bdadyslexia.org.uk*

Career Development Loans, Tel 0800 585 505.

www.lifelonglearning.org.uk has more details.

Learndirect: Call 0800 100 900 for information as outlined above or 0808 100 9000 in Scotland.

National Extension College, Michael Young Centre, Purbeck Road, Cambridge CB2 2HN, Tel 01223 400 200. Provides a range of correspondence courses including GCSEs, A levels, degree and higher education, career and business skills, counselling and guidance. *www.nec.ac.uk*

National Institute of Adult Continuing Education, Renaissance House, 20 Princess Road West, Leicester LE1 6TP. Tel 0116 204 4200. In Wales contact NIACE, Dysgu, Cymru, Third floor, 35 Cathedral Road, Cardiff CF11 9HB. Tel 0292 037 0900 or visit *www.niace.org.uk*

Open University, Central Enquiries, PO Box 200, Milton Keynes MK7 6AA. Tel 01908 653 231, *www.open.ac.uk*

UCAS, Rosehill, New Barn Lane, Cheltenham, Gloucestershire GL52 3LZ. Tel 08701 122211, *www.ucas.com* It has information for mature students, including on where to start, how to apply, what happens after you've applied and financial advice.

WEA (Workers' Educational Authority). For information about courses in your area, call Freephone 0800 328 1060,

www.wea.org.uk
www.hotcourses.com for lots of information about
out the country. If you want to acquire skills ba
particularly useful.

Job hunting

Jobcentre Plus. Check your *Yellow Pages* but also log onto
www.jobcentreplus.gov.uk to find your nearest job centre plus.
New Deal – *www.newdeal.gov.uk* or visit your local Jobcentre Plus
for more information.
Working for a Charity NCVO, Regent's Wharf, 8 All Saints Street,
London N1 9RL, Tel 020 7520 2512, *www.workingforacharity.or-
g.uk* Send an A4 SAE for information on working for charities or
email at *workingforacharity@ncvo-vol.org.uk*
These web sites may be useful:
www.fish4jobs.co.uk
www.jobsite.co.uk
www.manpower.co.uk
www.reed.co.uk
www.getalife.org.uk for information on working in the public sector
For recruitment agencies in your area, check also in *Yellow Pages*
under Recruitment and Employment Agencies.

Running your own business

The British Franchise Association, Thames View, Newtown Road,
Henley-On-Thames, Oxfordshire RG9 1HG. Tel 01491 578 049.
Offers help and advice in evaluating franchise offers; information
guide and franchise manual for a fee. *www.british-franchise.org.uk*
Business Link:
England: Business Link, visit *www.businesslink.gov.uk* or call
0845 600 9006
Wales: Business Eye at *www.businesseye.org.uk* or call 0845 796
9798

Lowland Scotland: Business Gateway at *www.bgateway.com* or call 0845 609 6611

Highlands & Islands: Highlands and Islands Enterprise at *www.hie.co.uk* or call 01463 234 171

Northern Ireland: Invest Northern Ireland at *www.investni.com* or call 028 90 23 90 90

Employers Helpline. Tel 08457 143 143. Can help with basic tax matters or national insurance enquiries. Also provides basic information on registering for VAT, statutory sick pay and maternity benefits. If you're thinking of taking someone on for the first time, call the New Employers Helpline on 0845 915 4515 for information.

Federation of Small Businesses, Sir Frank Whittle Way, Blackpool Business Park, Blackpool, Lancashire FY4 2FE. Tel: 01253 336000. Keep in touch with the issues which concern you and your business at *www.fsb.org.uk*

Inland Revenue – Now HM Revenue and Customs. For all matters relating to tax, PAYE, expenses and benefits, visit the substantial web site at *www.hmrc.gov.uk* To speak to someone in Welsh, call 0845 302 1489.

Being self employed, visit *www.hmrc.gov.uk/startingup* or call the helpline 08459 15 45 15.

New Deal for those wishing to set up their own business: Tel: 0845 606 2626 or visit *www.newdeal.gov.uk* or visit your local Job Centre Plus and ask to meet with an adviser.

Startups at *www.startups.co.uk* with lots of information on a huge range of subjects including IT security, raising finance, buying and selling a business, working from home.

Shell LiveWIRE scheme for those under 30 who want to start up their own business visit www.shell-livewire.org.

The Telework Association: Promotes teleworking and has advice on how to approach it, information on technology and lots more. Visit *www.tca.org.uk*

Being a social entrepreneur

Community Action Network, 1st Floor Downstream Building, 1
London Bridge, London SE1 9BG, Tel 0845 456 2537 or visit
www.can-online.org.uk – the UK's leading organisation for the
development and promotion of social entrepreneurs.

The School for Social Entrepreneurs has a web site at *www.sse.org.uk*

UnLtd – the Foundation for Social Entrepreneurs, a new charitable
organisation set up by seven leading non-profit organisations
(including Community Action Network) who promote social
entrepreneurship. Visit *www.unltd.org.uk*

Social enterprise

Social Enterprise Coalition – *www.socialenterprise.org.uk*

Voluntary work

National Centre for Volunteering, *www.volunteering.org.uk*

TimeBank: Tel: 0845 601 4008, *www.timebank.org.uk*

Caring for others

Carers UK, 20-25 Glasshouse Yard, London EC1A 4JT, Freephone
0808 808 77 77 from 10:00-12:00am and 2:00-4:00pm Wednesday
and Thursday. Visit *www.carersuk.org* for more information.

Carers UK Back Me Up: For a list of Careers Emergency Schemes, call
020 7566 7617 or visit *www.careersuk.org/backmeup*

Daycare Trust for help finding and choosing good quality childcare.
Tel 020 7840 3350 or visit *www.daycaretrust.org.uk*

Department for Work and Pensions enquiry line for carers and
disabled people: 0800 882 200 or visit *www.dwp.gov.uk*

4Children, City Reach, 5 Greenwich View Place, London E14 9NN,
for information on out-of-school clubs. Tel 020 7512 2100 or visit

www.4children.org.uk, or you can email them at *info@4children.org.uk*

Lone Parents

Child Support Agency, National Enquiry Line: Tel: 08457 133 133, *www.csa.gov.uk/*

Gingerbread, 7 Sovereign Close, Sovereign Court, London E1W 2HW. Call the Advice Line and Membership Freephone: 0800 018 4318. Visit their web site at
www.gingerbread.org.uk

www.newdeal.gov.uk for information on the New Deal Scheme for lone parents.

Parents

Caring for a Family: 209-211 City Road, London EC1V 1JN. Call 020 7608 8700 or visit *www.cafamily.org.uk*. A national charity for parents and professionals involved with or caring for a child with any disability, including rare disorders. Brings families together through a network of local and national mutual support and self-help groups.

Working Families: Visit *www.workingfamlies.org.uk* or call 0800 0130313. Lots of useful information on your rights at work, flexible working, childcare, low income parents, help for fathers, and new parents.

Raising Kids: *www.raisingkids.co.uk* a great web site with lots of useful information on raising children and handling life.

Other useful addresses

Commission for Racial Equality, St Dunstan's House, 201-211 Borough High Street, London SE1 1GZ. Tel 020 7939 0000 or visit *www.cre.gov.uk*

Department for Work and Pensions: *www.dwp.gov.uk* – a huge site with details on all aspects of work and benefits.

Equal Opportunities Commission, Arndale House, Arndale Centre, Manchester M4 3EQ. Tel: 08456 015901, *www.eoc.org.uk*

Health and Safety Executive Information Line. Gives information and provides publications on a wide range of business health and safety issues. *www.hse.gov.uk*

 ## For Women

These web site cover all sorts of issues relating to women, including jobs and careers:

www.femail.co.uk The Daily Mail Web site

www.ivillage.co.uk/workcareer

www.women-returners.co.uk

www.everywoman.co.uk – a great networking organisation for businesswomen

www.wireuk.org – Women In Rural Enterprises, a networking and business club to help you start and maintain your own rural enterprise

 ## Specialist Support Groups

Access to Work Scheme: *www.jobcentreplus.gov.uk* A scheme provided through disability employment advisors which gives practical advice and support to disabled people and their employers to help overcome work-related obstacles resulting from any disability. There are other schemes. Your local JobCentre Plus office will have details.

Apex Charitable Trust, St Alphage House, Wingate Annexe, 2 Fore Street, London EC2Y 5DA, Tel: 020 7638 5931 or visit *www.apex-trust.com* The Apex Trust helps people with criminal records find appropriate employment or start up on their own by building the right skills and breaking down barriers to employment.

British Heart Foundation: Heart Information Line at 08450 70 80 70
or visit *www.bhf.org.uk*

Cancer Free Helpline: 0808 800 1234 or visit
www.cancerbacup.org.uk/

Disability Alliance, Universal House, 88-94 Wentworth Street,
London E1 7SA, Tel: 020 7247 8776; minicom 002 7247 8776 or
visit *www.disabilityalliance.org* – has information on all aspects of
disability, including benefits, tax credits and community care.

National Association for the Care and Resettlement of Offenders
(NACRO), 169 Clapham Road, London SW9 0PU, Tel: 020 7582
6500 or visit *www.nacro.org.uk*

Skill, 4th Floor, Chapter House, 18-20 Crucifix Lane, London SE1
3JW. Tel: information service 0800 328 5050; minicom 0800 068
2422. Helps those with disabilities or learning difficulties. You can
visit their web site at *www.skill.org.uk*

Ageism

www.agepostiive.gov.uk – the Government web site.

Employers Forum on Age, Floor 3, Downstream, 1 London Bridge,
London SE1 9BG. Tel: 0845 456 2495 or visit
www.efa.org.uk

Maturity Works: *www.maturityworks.co.uk* – lots of practical advice
and tips for the mature job seeker, plus case studies highlighting
benefits of taking on mature workers.

Work life balance

www.employersforwork-lifebalance.org.uk run by the Work Foundation.

The Personal Finance Society at *www.thepfs.org/* – a database of
independent financial advisers.

 **Future Focused**

The Pre-Retirement Association of Great Britain and Northern Ireland, 9 Chesham Road, Guildford, Surrey GU1 3LS, Tel: 01483 301170. Runs course in mid-life planning, helps people take stock and make changes.

Index

TIGHT UP-SKIRT.
sweetie me nadia rose

There once was a beautiful, intelligent sexy kind Robot called Adeola Johnson. Adeola Johnson had strong political convictions and wanted to see a free world for all people. Adeola listened to revolutionary + inspiring music and interpreters of that music. Tonight she listened to the astonishing sounds of Stax with the incomparable Booker T, the sensitive and soulful Beverley Knight, the wonderful William Bell and the clever Steve Cropper. Sometimes - sometime she Adeola couldn't afford the astronomically priced tickets. Sam Moore was always an aural delight. Adeola wanted wanted to emulate Beverley for her talent, perseverance and energy. Throughout the years Beverley toiled long and hard until she reached the glorious musical heights of performing with two soul gods Tom Jones and Sam Moore. Such an accolade befits a goddess which she is. Adeola asked Good God Almighty to find a way to emulate Beverley's musical milestones.

If you want to know how ... to practise psychometric tests

'The good news is there are thousands of brilliant firms out there, offering everything from sky-high salaries, profit-related bonuses, long holidays, flexible working, career-enhancing training schemes, staff discounts, free canteens, health and life insurance, gyms, outings, holidays ... you name it. But first you'll have to get in.

Unfortunately the days when all you needed was a great CV and a sparkling performance at interview are long gone. Now you also need to be able to pass a whole range of psychometric and management tests with flying colours. That's what this book is all about.'

Andrea Shavick

Practice Psychometric Tests
How to familiarise yourself with genuine recruitment tests and get the job you want
Andrea Shavick

Following the success of Andrea Shavick's *Passing Psychometric Tests* and *Psychometric Tests for Graduates* comes this book, crammed full of even more genuine practice psychometric tests from SHL Group plc, the biggest test publisher in the world. They are the tests used by over 95% of the FTSE 100 companies to select their staff, as do the police, the Civil Service, the Armed Forces ... the list is endless. So if you're looking for a job, you need this book!

ISBN 1 84528 020 2

Eddee Flayd

If you want to know how ... to prepare for interviews

'It's the interviewer's prerogative to throw just about any question they can think of at the interviewee. So you might think that it's almost impossible to prepare for an interview. But the truth is that 80% of interview questions revolve around 20 common themes. And many interviewees let themselves down by not thinking about these themes, preparing and rehearsing responses to them.

'Many candidates then go on to create a wrong impression. Remember that an interviewer has to *like* you and warm to you as a person, as well as want to work with you because you answer the questions well. I see too many candidates who talk too much or come across as nervous or unfriendly. If you get the chance to rehearse with a friend and get some feedback on just how you come across, you will improve your chances no end.'

Rob Yeung

Successful Interviews Every Time
Rob Yeung

'*Successful Interviews* is the type of book that one may not wish to share with others who are job seeking in competition with oneself. Nevertheless, I owe a debt of gratitude to Dr Rob Yeung for sharing his experiences with us...' *S. Lewis, Coventry*

'This book is an invaluable source of information for job hunters on preparing for interviews, tests and assessment centres.' *Jonathan Turpin, Chief Executive of job hunting website fish4jobs.co.uk*

ISBN 1 85703 978 5

If you want to know how ... to write a great CV

'At some time, we are all likely to need a CV. Whether we're leaving school or college, wanting a career change, experiencing redundancy or returning from a career break, our first priority is to get a CV written. Not only is a CV necessary for the benefit of the intended reader, but as this book will illustrate, compiling one can provide a great insight for you personally. Rather than relying on someone who doesn't know you to write your "personal sales brochure", this book gives you a practical step-by-step approach to creating your own.'

Paul McGee

Write a Great CV
Prepare a powerful CV that really works
Paul McGee

This book will help you get your foot in the door and get that interview. You know you can do the job you're going for, but how do you convince the person you are applying to? What you need is a well-designed CV, and that's where this book will help.

Paul McGee provides insights and tips gained from helping thousands of people from all ages and backgrounds to market themselves successfully.

'This book contains useful specimen CVs, covering letters and case studies, together with sample jobs, action plans and interview preparation tips.' *Office Secretary*

ISBN 1 85703 754 5

If you want to know how ... to use computers in the workplace

'There are hundreds of books on computing and IT in the bookshops, but very few are aimed specifically at those in general or administrative positions or, particularly, women returning to work. Having trained hundreds of office workers and women returners, it became clear to me that a single book was needed covering every aspect of general computing that you are likely to face.

Hopefully this book will give you the confidence and provide all the guidance you need to carry out the many and varied tasks you may be asked to perform.'

Jackie Sherman

Essential Computing Skills for Working Women or Returners
Everything you need to know to use computers in the workplace
Jackie Sherman

This book is for anyone either starting in, or returning to, the workplace and worried about their computer skills. It can be used:

- To feel confident you are computer literate
- To make sure you are up to date
- To keep as a reference guide
- To be ready for an unfamiliar task
- To work confidently with shared files

and much more!

ISBN 1 84528 054 7

If you want to know how ... to successfully apply for a job

'Being successful in a fiercely competitive jobs market takes time and effort. Spurring a recruiter into wanting to know more about you is the secret of success with any application. Each one must be special: it has to say "Here I am. This is what I can offer you." This book is designed to help you present your skills in a practical and marketable manner and ultimately achieve your goal. How you approach this crucial first stage is vitally important, only successful applications lead to interviews.'

Judith Johnstone

The Job Application Handbook
A systematic guide to applying for a job
Judith Johnstone

Whether you're leaving university, re-entering the job market, facing redundancy or simply wanting a change, this handbook reveals the best ways to approach potential employers.

'A great buy. It reiterates points which need to be repeated and gives practical advice on job finding.' – *Office Secretary Magazine*

'Laden with common sense ... particularly useful for first-timers.' – *MC, University College Dublin*

ISBN 1 85703 992 0

Ruby Turner
I'll Take You There

Sir tom Jones

How To Books are available through all good bookshops, or you can order direct from us through Grantham Book Services.

Tel: +44 (0)1476 541080
Fax: +44 (0)1476 541061
Email: orders@gbs.tbs-ltd.co.uk

Or via our website

www.howtobooks.co.uk

To order via any of these methods please quote the title(s) of the book(s) and your credit card number together with its expiry date.

For further information about our books and catalogue, please contact:

How To Books
Spring Hill House
Spring Hill Road
Begbroke
Oxford OX5 1RX

Visit our web site at

www.howtobooks.co.uk

Or you can contact us by email at info@howtobooks.co.uk